Android Animations by Tutorials

By Filip Babić, Prateek Prasad & Alex Sullivan

Android Animations by Tutorials

Filip Babić, Prateek Prasad & Alex Sullivan

Notice of Rights

Notice of Liability

Trademarks

ISBN: 978-1-950325-56-6

Table of Contents

Book License

By purchasing *Android Animations by Tutorials*, you have the following license:

- You are allowed to use and/or modify the source code in *Android Animations by Tutorials* in as many apps as you want, with no attribution required.
- You are allowed to use and/or modify all art, images and designs that are included in *Android Animations by Tutorials* in as many apps as you want, but must include this attribution line somewhere inside your app: "Artwork/images/designs: from *Android Animations by Tutorials*, available at www.raywenderlich.com".
- The source code included in *Android Animations by Tutorials* is for your personal use only. You are NOT allowed to distribute or sell the source code in *Android Animations by Tutorials* without prior authorization.
- This book is for your personal use only. You are NOT allowed to sell this book without prior authorization, or distribute it to friends, coworkers or students; they would need to purchase their own copies.

All materials provided with this book are provided on an "as is" basis, without warranty of any kind, express or implied, including but not limited to the warranties of merchantability, fitness for a particular purpose and noninfringement. In no event shall the authors or copyright holders be liable for any claim, damages or other liability, whether in an action of contract, tort or otherwise, arising from, out of or in connection with the software or the use or other dealings in the software.

All trademarks and registered trademarks appearing in this guide are the properties of their respective owners.

Before You Begin

This section tells you a few things you need to know before you get started, such as what you'll need for hardware and software, where to find the project files for this book, and more.

What You Need

To follow along with this book, you'll need the following:

- A computer capable of running Android Studio (Windows, Mac or Linux). See https://developer.android.com/studio/ for more specific requirements.
- **Device or Emulator that Supports Android 9.0 or Greater**: If you want to test on actual devices, you'll need one or more Android devices. However, all the examples in the book will run using the Emulator included with Android Studio.
- **Kotlin 1.5**: Because Jetpack Compose relies on a special Kotlin compiler, you need Kotlin 1.5 or later both to write the code and for the compiler to process special Jetpack Compose annotations.
- **Android Studio Artic Fox**: This IDE is up to date with all the tools you will need.

Book Source Code & Forums

Where to download the materials for this book

The materials for this book can be cloned or downloaded from the GitHub book materials repository:

- https://github.com/raywenderlich/aat-materials/tree/editions/1.0

Forums

We've also set up an official forum for the book at https://forums.raywenderlich.com/c/books/android-animations-by-tutorials. This is a great place to ask questions about the book or to submit any errors you may find.

"I would like to thank my friends, family and my loved one for the continuous support that you give me each day, when I throw myself into huge projects that challenge me. People can do anything we set our minds to, but without others to remind us of that, we can't fully realize that potential. I'd like to thank my mentor Marijan for all the positivity you've planted in my head, showing how much I'm capable of with a little shift of perspective."

— Filip Babić

"To my wonderful parents. Thank you for encouraging, supporting and at times enduring me. This is all for you!"

— Prateek Prasad

"To my wonderful partner Pallavi, without whom I would have never been able to start this undertaking. Your support and encouragement mean the world to me."

— Alex Sullivan

About the Authors

Prateek Prasad is an engineer and a product designer. He specializes in building mobile apps and has been doing so ever since high school. He also mentors beginners in the tech industry on OpenClassrooms. In his free time, he likes playing music or nerding out about outer space.

Filip Babić is a senior Android developer from Croatia, and a Google Developer Expert for Android & Kotlin. He's currently focusing on Jetpack Compose and Kotlin Coroutines and building awesome things with those tools. While doing so, he's teaching people about topics in Android and Kotlin and sharing his knowledge in various types of community engagement.

Alex Sullivan Alex is a freelance mobile developer in Boston who loves to work on native Android, iOS, React Native, and Flutter apps. He's a big fan of reactive programming and learning about new ways to create silky-smooth Android and iOS apps. In his spare time, he enjoys reading, playing video games and rewatching Star Trek: The Next Generation for the billionth time.

About the Editors

Antonio Roa-Valverde is the tech editor of this book. Antonio is a software engineer specialized in Android development. He's interested in innovation and shaping new products with potential impact on people. Google Developer Group co-organizer in Innsbruck and Munich.You can find him close to the mountains, either hiking, riding the mountain-bike or catching some curvy roads by motorcycle.

Sandra Grauschopf is the editor of this book. Sandra is a writer, editor, and content strategist as well as the Book Team Lead at raywenderlich.com. She loves to untangle tortured sentences and to travel the world with a trusty book in her hand. You can follow her on LinkedIn or learn more about her at grauschopf.com.

Jennifer Bailey is a former software engineer who is now a full-time professor for Aims Community College in Colorado where she teaches mobile app development for Android and iOS. She also teaches courses in Python, Java, C++, and .NET platform utilizing C#. She is the lead organizer of Google Developer Group of Northern Colorado. She enjoys various Android meetups and conferences around the United States. In her spare time, Jenn enjoys rollerblading, horseback riding and spending time with her teenage daughter, dogs and cats.

Introduction

Animating an app is clearly one of the most rewarding, fun and effective ways to enhance the user interface of your android apps. Animations provide visual cues to your users that make the interface fun and easy to use. They give your app a unique flair that make it memoriable and appealing. Everyone enjoys using an app that employs strategic use of animations. They can draw the user's eye to important parts of the interface, or just add some visual excitement into the design.

You've probably seen some impressive animation effects in some of your favorite apps. Effective use of animations means using many different types of animations, from more subtle effects to impressive large animations that really make the content explode from the screen. As an app creator in the Android platform, you'll need to learn about a lot of different types of animations.

In this book you'll discover and use many of the most common types of animations found in Android apps today. These include simple view and property animations, transition animations, animating lists and list gestures and even a taste of the popular Jetpack Compose animations. With an arsenal of knowledge like this, you'll be able to incorporate awesome animations into critical parts of your own apps. By the end of the book after working through the chapters and tackling the challenges at the end, you'll have gained hands-on experience using a wide array of different types of animations for every occassion.

Are you ready to jump in?

How to read this book

In this book, each chapter will start with the same starter app. This will allow you to really focus on one type of animation at a time while keeping the code less complicated. It also means that you can do the chapters in any order that you please. So don't hesitate to roll up your sleeves and try whichever animations you'd like. While reading this book, be sure to work through the steps and examine the code samples, and you are encouraged to attempt the challenges as well. The solutions to the challenges are provided in the sample code.

This book is split into four main sections:

Section I: View & Property Animations

In section one, you will begin by learning about the most basic types of animations. You'll learn how to use **ValueAnimator** and **ObjectAnimator** to provide subtle yet meaningful cues to your users. These tools will allow you to to animate the properties of your views. You'll also learn about the different types of **Interpolators** that control the rate of change on an animated property.

You'll learn how to apply animations not only to the standard views in the UI tookit, but also how to animate custom views. This will include a demonstration of how to decouple the animation from the internal handling to keep the code structured properly. Oftentimes, you'll want to reverse an animation, this is included in this section as well.

Last but not least, you'll get to learn all about XML Animations. XML animations are very convenient to use and render your animation code reusable. You'll learn about the difference between the **anim** and **animator** directories, and when to use each one. The knowledge you gain from this section will help you make more informed decisions about which animations to choose when adding animations in your own app.

Section II: Screen Transitions

In this section, you'll learn about one of the most important types of animations found in an app, transitions. Screen transitions help your user understand where they are at when moving from one activity or fragment to another. You'll begin by animating transitions with XML animations. You'll see the different types of navigation component fragment animations and learn how to apply complex transitions between activities and fragments utilizing animation sets.

Then, you'll learn how to apply animations to specific views during a transition using the **Transition Framework**. This will allow you to make even more complex and intriguing transitions between fragments and activities. You'll also get a primer on how to troubleshoot some of the most common pitfalls you'll run into when utilizig the transition framework.

Lastly, and most exciting, you'll learn about **Element Transitions**. This allows a transition to center the focus around a shared element between two fragments and does not require transitioning the whole view heirarcy. Instead, the shared element takes the center stage and becomes a powerful visual effect. You'll learn how to do a circular reveal to reveal tab content, and how to use custom transitions to make the transition look attractive.

Section III: List & Gesture Animations

In this section you'll learn how to use another crucial type of animation for your app, List Animations and Gestures. First, you will work with basic list animations in a recyclerview. You'll use **ItemAnimator** to animate the creation, reordering and removal of items in a list. You'll take a close look at utilizing **DiffUtil** with the **ListAdapter** to emit intelligent changes to the dataset.

You'll then move on to **ItemTouchHelper** animations which animate the items as the user swipes them off or rearranges the items of a list using drag and drop gestures. You'll learn how to enable gestures on a list to detect swiping and drag and drop reording of items. You'll use **item resetting** to visually alert the user that they've added an item. Your app will allow users to reorder items with drag and drop in style.

Finally, you'll learn how to incorporate animations while the user is scrolling items in a list. You'll set up scroll listeners, detect the scrolling gestures and how far the list has been scrolled, and respond by updating the UI when scrolling. You'll learn how to show and hide UI components when scrolling, and how to use **CoordinatorLayout** with a **CollapsingToolbarLayout** to acheive a stunning paralax effect when the user scrolls.

Section IV: Jetpack Compose Animations

As a final treat, this section will take you through an overview of Jetpack Compose animations. Utilizing **AnimatedVisibilty** you'll be able to look at the state and determine the visibility of the **Composable**s wrapped within it. You'll learn how to use different types of animations like slide-in or fade-in, and how to apply multiple animations at a time. You'll also learn about animating the properties of views such as size or color, and how to animate the state changes in your app.

Section I: View & Property Animations

In section one, you will begin by learning about the most basic types of animations. You'll learn how to use ValueAnimator and ObjectAnimator to provide subtle yet meaningful cues to your users. These tools will allow you to to animate the properties of your views. You'll also learn about the different types of Interpolators that control the rate of change on an animated property. You'll learn how to apply animations not only to the standard views in the UI tookit, but also how to animate custom views. This will include a demonstration of how to decouple the animation from the internal handling to keep the code structured properly. Oftentimes, you'll want to reverse an animation, this is included in this section as well.

Last but not least, you'll get to learn all about XML Animations. XML animations are very convenient to use and render your animation code reusable. You'll learn about the difference between the anim and animator directories, and when to use each one. The knowledge you gain from this section will help you make more informed decisions about which animations to choose when adding animations in your own app.

Chapter 1: Value & Object Animators

By Prateek Prasad

As smartphones have grown in power and capability over the years, users' expectations of mobile apps have changed as well. Today's apps don't just need to be functional and performant; they also need to offer an elegant UI and a fabulous user experience.

Animations play a crucial part in offering a good user experience for mobile apps. When used correctly and in the proper context, animations add immense value to the user. They can offer subtle visual cues about a task, like indicating a file upload failed or notifying users when the screen's data changes. You can also leverage animations to transition between different screens, signifying continuity.

Android offers a variety of ways to create animations, and each section of this book focuses on a specific animation category. In this first chapter, you'll learn about one of the simplest ways of animating views: by using **ValueAnimator** and **ObjectAnimator**.

Setting up the project

To start writing your first animation, open the starter project for this chapter in **Android Studio**.

In this book, you'll work on a movie review app called **Cinematic**.

Build and run the project. You'll get your first glimpse of Cinematic:

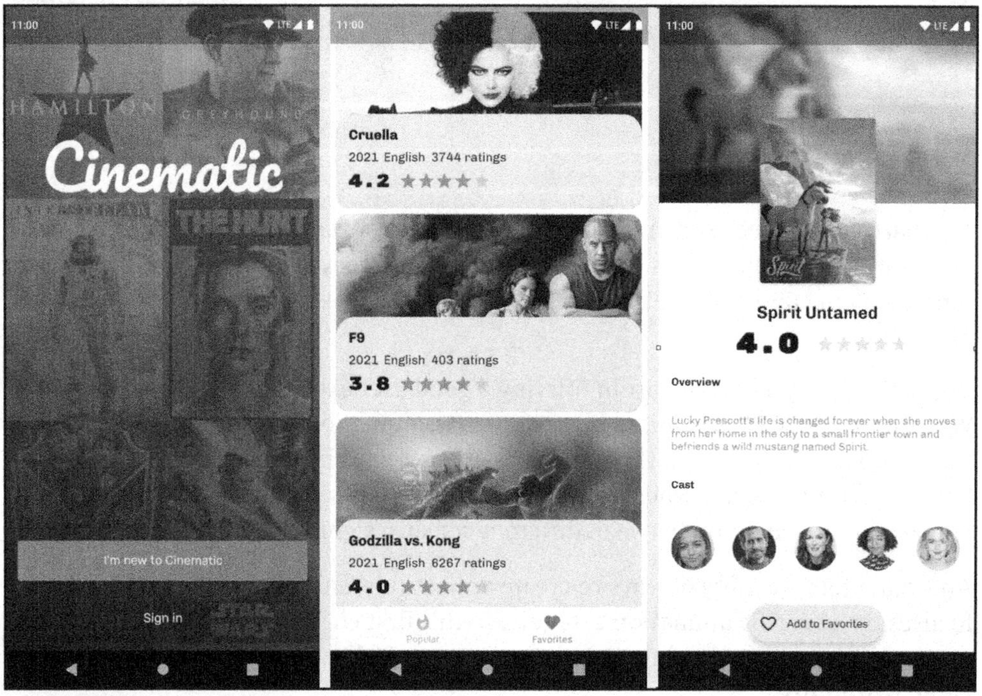

The app has three distinct features:

- **Authentication**: Mimics the standard signup and login flow.
- **Main feed**: A tabbed screen showing you a list of popular movies and movies you've added to your list of favorites.
- **Details screen**: Tapping a movie takes you to the details screen, which shows you more information including the movie's synopsis and cast list.

The project is a standard **MVVM-based** app that uses Modern Android Development best practices.

Expand the project view in Android Studio to look at the package structure for the project:

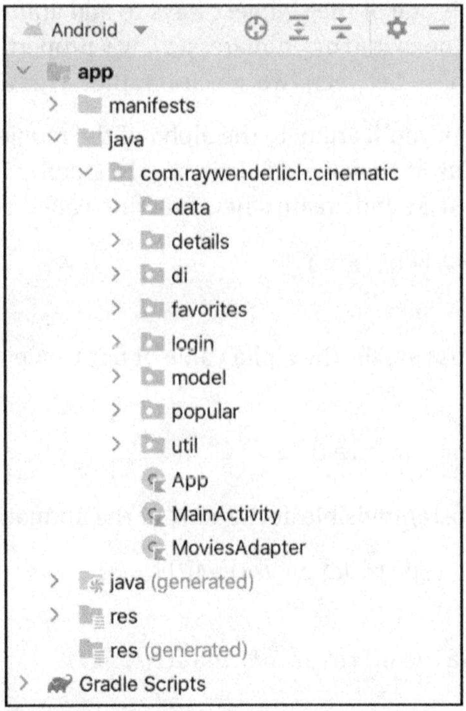

- **di**: Sets up dependency injection for the project using Koin. You can learn more about using this framework with our Dependency Injection With Koin course: https://www.raywenderlich.com/9457-dependency-injection-with-koin.
- **model**: Defines all the models that the various screens of the app use.
- **data**: Contains the repository setup that the main screen and the details screen use to fetch data about movies. To keep things simple and for consistency, the project uses a prepopulated database for the movie data.
- **util**: Contains several utility classes and extensions.
- **favorites**: Holds classes related to the **favorites** screen.
- **popular**: Contains classes related to the **popular** screen.
- **details**: Contains classes related to the **details** screen.

Now that you've had a quick walkthrough of the app and the project, it's time to write your very first animation. :]

Exploring ValueAnimator

Using ValueAnimator is one of the simplest ways to add animations on Android. As the name suggests, ValueAnimator animates a view's properties — for example, its rotation, scale and alpha — between two specific values over time.

For your first animation, you'll animate the alpha of the movie poster in **MovieDetailsFragment.kt** to make it fade in slowly. Open **MovieDetailsFragment.kt** and create a new function called animatePoster().

```
private fun animatePoster() {
}
```

Next, inside animatePoster, set the alpha value of posterContainer to **0**, as shown below:

```
binding.posterContainer.alpha = 0f
```

This code makes the poster invisible at the start of the animation.

Next, add the following code to set up ValueAnimator:

```
// 1
val animator = ValueAnimator.ofFloat(0f, 1f)
animator.duration = 1000
// 2
animator.addUpdateListener { valueAnimator ->
  // 3
  val animatedValue = valueAnimator.animatedValue as Float
  // 4
  binding.posterContainer.alpha = animatedValue
}
// 5
animator.start()
```

Here's a breakdown of what's going on above:

1. You instantiated a new ValueAnimator using the static method ofFloat. ofFloat accepts two floating values, and the view's properties animate between them. Here, you specified a **start value** of **0** and an **end value** of **1**. The duration specifies how long this animation will run. In this case, it's **1000**, which indicates 1,000 milliseconds or one second.

2. You added an UpdateListener() to the animator. The animator calls the update listener after every update to the animated value.

3. Here, you retrieved the current animated value from the animator and cast it to a `Float`.
4. You then used the current value to set the poster's alpha value.
5. Finally, you started the animation.

Before you can play this animation, you need to replace the `TODO` item in `loadPoster()` and call the newly created `animatePoster()`.

```
animatePoster()
```

Now, build and run. Tap a movie card to open the **details** screen. You'll notice the movie poster slowly fades into view:

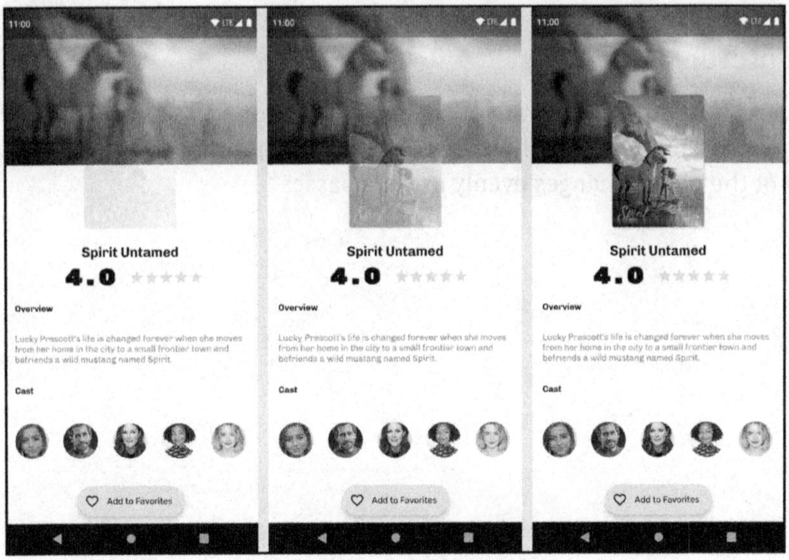

Awesome job writing your first animation!

Before you proceed, it's worth spending time to understand the internals of how this animation — and animations in general! — work. You'll do that next.

Understanding interpolators

The human eye retains images for a short period, even when the image itself is no longer there. This phenomenon is called **persistence of vision**. Videos exploit this attribute of our eyes to give us a sense of motion when we're actually seeing a collection of still images, strategically stitched together.

The images that make up a video are called **frames**. When an object in the video is changing, this object will be slightly different in each frame.

Animations use a similar premise. First, you define which properties of an object you want to change. Then, you specify the value by which they change and how long it should take for the change to occur. **Interpolators** control the rate at which each property of a view changes during an animation. In simplified terms, an animation is just a mathematical timing function defined by the rate at which the given property of an object changes.

Android offers a whole suite of interpolators to fit your needs. Based on the one you choose, your animation can range from subtle, to dramatic.

You'll learn about some of the most common interpolators next.

Linear interpolator

In the linear interpolator, the rate of change of the property's value stays constant with time. You can use a straight line on a graph to represent this motion. The position of the object changes evenly as time passes.

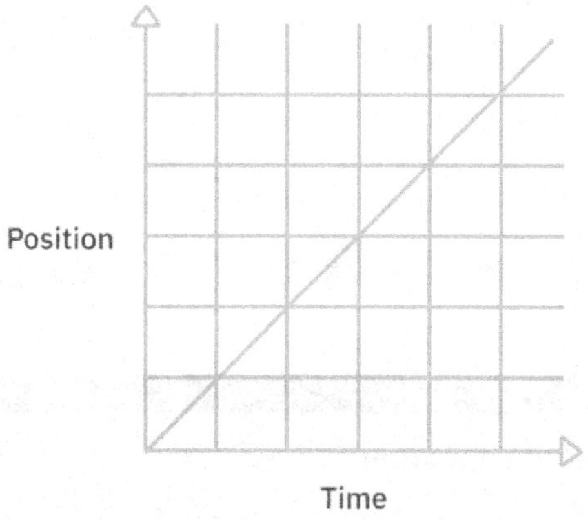

With linear interpolation, animations can end up feeling robotic. In the real world, motion is never linear because friction and other forces influence objects in motion. It's best to avoid linear interpolators if you want your animations to feel natural.

Accelerate interpolator

In the accelerate interpolator, the rate of change of the property's value starts slow and accelerates over time.

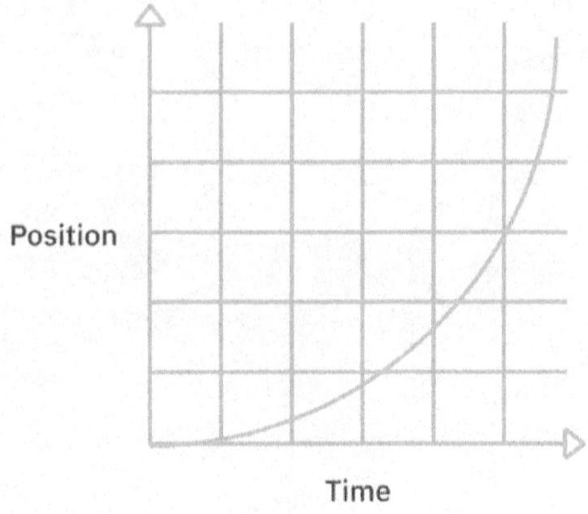

A good example of an accelerated motion would be a car that starts off slow but goes faster once you hit the gas.

Decelerate interpolator

The decelerate interpolator is the opposite of the accelerate interpolator. In the decelerate interpolator, the rate of change of the property's value starts fast and decelerates over time.

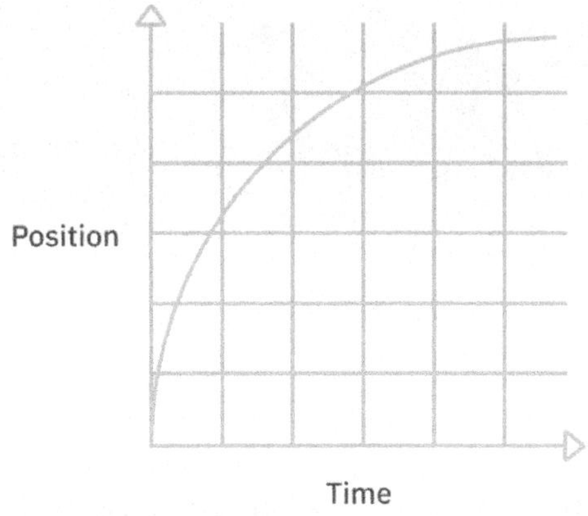

Deceleration is quite common in the real world. To visualize the timing curve, think about a ball that you roll on the floor. It starts off fast but slows down over time, eventually coming to a stop.

AccelerateDecelerate interpolator

The AccelerateDecelerate interpolator is a combination of the accelerate and the decelerate interpolator. The rate of change of the property's value starts slow, speeds up in the middle and ends slow.

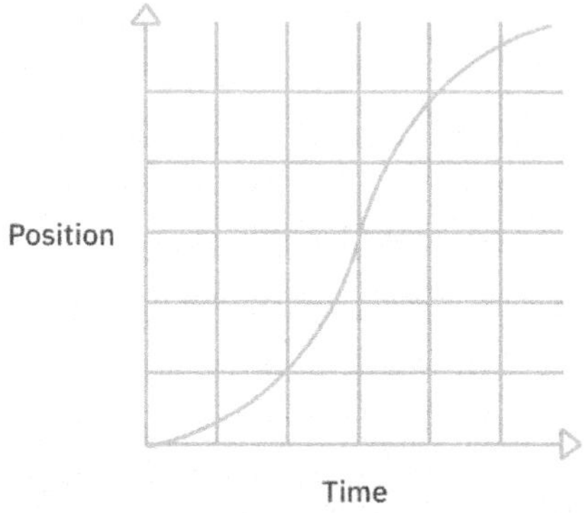

This is another type of motion pattern that is very common in the real world. Any object that starts off moving fast, slows down and eventually comes to a halt. Think of the motion of a pendulum swing.

Overshoot interpolator

The overshoot interpolator accelerates the property value change, goes beyond the final specified value then, finally, decelerates.

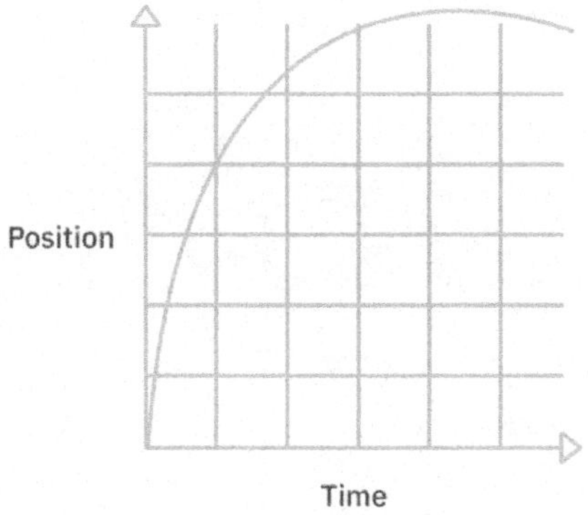

Overshoot is one of the more dramatic interpolators in Android. For a good visualization of this kind of motion, think back to any cartoon from your childhood where a leashed dog tried to chase something.The dog goes slightly beyond its leash length and gets pulled back at the end.

Anticipate interpolator

The anticipate interpolator is the opposite of the interpolator. It starts by changing the property's value to go below the starting value, then accelerates it. One way to use it is to give a dramatic exit effect.

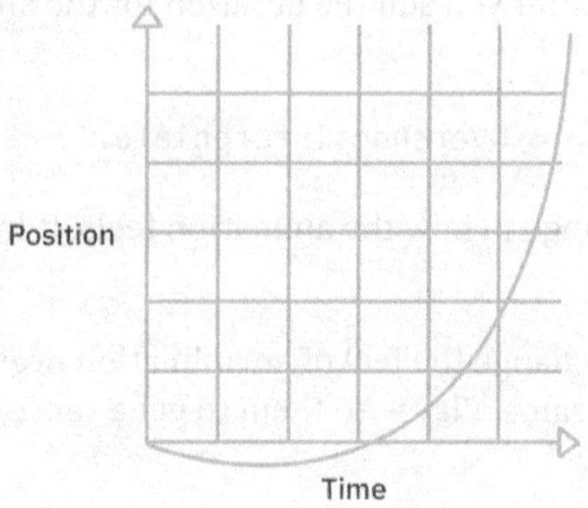

The anticipate timing curve is similar to a slingshot — the object is pulled back, and then it shoots off.

Bounce interpolator

In a bounce interpolator, the animation ends in a bounce. Imagine an eraser falling, bouncing slightly when it hits the floor, then settling.

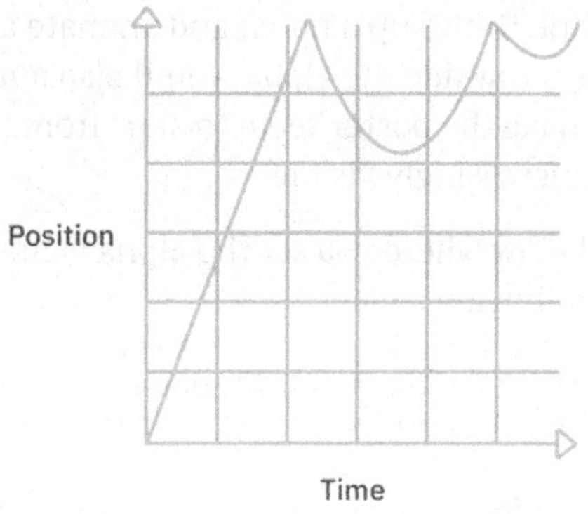

Android offers a few more interpolators. You can learn more about them in Android's interpolator documentation (https://developer.android.com/reference/android/view/animation/Interpolator).

Using interpolators

Now that you have a theoretical understanding of interpolators, it's time to use them in your animations. You'll start by adding an interpolator to the poster.

In `animatePoster()`, right after you add the duration for the animation, add the following line:

```
animator.interpolator = OvershootInterpolator()
```

Build and run to see the change in how the animation feels. It looks great, doesn't it?

> **Note**: Interpolators can change the feel of an animation even when its property values stay the same. Play with them to get a sense of what each one brings to the table.

So far, you've animated a single property of a view. Wouldn't it be fun to animate multiple properties at the same time? That's what you'll learn to do in the next section.

Animating multiple properties

For your next step, you'll crank things up a notch and animate another property of the poster. For this next one, alongside the alpha, you'll also animate the scale of the poster. This animation will make the poster seem to start from nothing, then grow slowly while also becoming increasingly visible.

In `animatePoster()`, right below where you set the alpha value to `posterContainer`, add the following code:

```
binding.posterContainer.scaleX = animatedValue
binding.posterContainer.scaleY = animatedValue
```

The code you just added will animate the scale of the view over time. It will start at a scale of **0** and gradually scale up to **1**.

Build and run. You'll see the effect in action. Pretty cool, right?

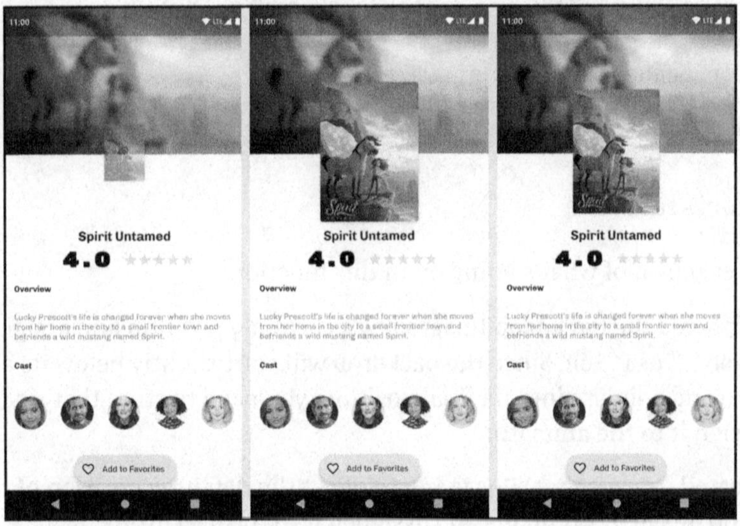

Animating the backdrop

Before you head on to learning about Object Animator, you'll add one more animation to the details screen.

Create a new function in **MovieDetailsFragment.kt** named `animateBackdrop`.

```
private fun animateBackdrop() {

}
```

Now, you'll animate the movie card's backdrop to subtly make it feel like it's sliding up from the bottom of the screen.

Add the following code inside `animateBackdrop`:

```
//1
val finalYPosition = binding.backdrop.y

//2
val startYPosition = finalYPosition + 40
binding.backdrop.y = startYPosition

//3
val animator = ValueAnimator.ofFloat(startYPosition,
finalYPosition)

//4
```

```
animator.duration = 1000
animator.interpolator = DecelerateInterpolator()

//5
animator.addUpdateListener { valueAnimator ->
  val animatedValue = valueAnimator.animatedValue as Float
  binding.backdrop.translationY = animatedValue
}
//6
animator.start()
```

Here's a breakdown of what's going on in this function:

1. You extracted the `backdrop` ImageView's current y position and assigned it to a new `finalYPosition`. Since the backdrop will start slightly below its actual position and animate into its final position, you need to store that final position and assign it to the animator.
2. You created a new `startYPosition` to offset the default y position of the backdrop image by **40 pixels** and assigned it to the backdrop.
3. Then, you instantiated a new `ValueAnimator` using the static method `ofFloat` and specified the start and end values via the `startYPosition` and `finalYPosition` properties.
4. You assigned **1000 milliseconds** for the animation duration and used a `DecelerateInterpolator`.
5. Here, you added an `updateListener()` to the animator. This listener gets the current `animatedValue` from the animator and casts it to a `Float`. It then uses the current value to set the backdrop's y translation value.
6. Finally, you started the animation.

Call `animateBackdrop()` from `loadBackdrop()` by replacing the `TODO`. Build and run. You'll see this subtle new addition to the details screen.

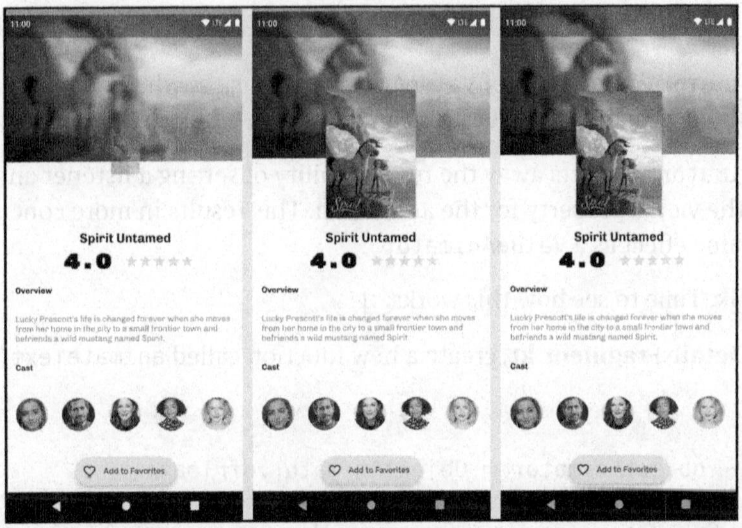

`ValueAnimator` is a powerful and flexible API that allows you to animate a view's properties reasonably easily. But it can quickly become too verbose when you want to animate multiple views on the screen.

`ValueAnimator` requires you to:

- Set up the animator.
- Specify the terminal values that the animator will work with.
- Set up `updateListener()` on the animator.
- Manipulate the view's properties based on the updated animation values.
- Give the animation a duration and start it.

This works well when you want to use a single animator to animate multiple properties of a view in one go, like when you used `animatePoster()` to animate the scale and the alpha of the poster. When you want to animate only a single property, however, it can get a little tedious. There's got to be a better way.

Animating single properties with ObjectAnimator

ObjectAnimator is a subclass of ValueAnimator. In cases where you only want to modify a single property of a view, it's a great choice.

ObjectAnimator abstracts away the responsibility of setting a listener and manually updating the view's property for the animation. This results in more concise code with the same effect as a ValueAnimator.

Enough talk. Time to see how this works. :]

In **MovieDetailsFragment.kt**, create a new function called animateText():

```
private fun animateText() {}
  //1
  val objectAnimator = ObjectAnimator.ofFloat(
    binding.summary,
    "alpha",
    0f,
    1f
  )

  //2
  objectAnimator.duration = 1000
  objectAnimator.start()
}
```

Here's what's going on:

1. You instantiated ObjectAnimator using the static function ofFloat(). Unlike ValueAnimator, the object takes two additional arguments: the view you want to animate, which is the summary TextView in this case, and the property of the view you wish to animate. Here, it's "alpha". Make sure you specify the name correctly, or the animation might not work.
2. You set the duration for this animation to **1,000 milliseconds** — that is, one second — and start the animation.

As a final step, call the newly created `animateText()` from `renderUI()` by replacing the `TODO` item.

```
animateText()
```

Build and run. Now, check out this slick and elegant animation that loads the summary of the movie.

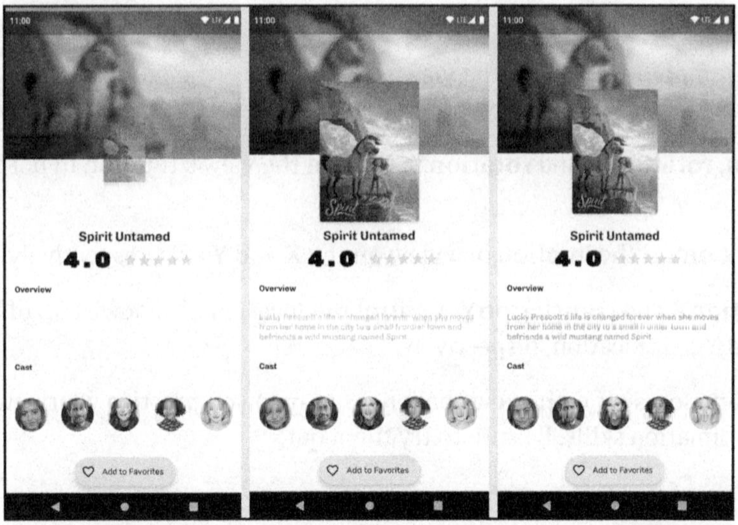

Wasn't that easy? `ObjectAnimator` is a strong option if you want to spice up a skin's UX quickly or attract the user's attention to something important on the screen.

Now that you've learned two ways to create animations, you might wonder which properties you can animate. You'll look at those next.

Animatable properties

The Value Animator API is extremely flexible. Because it gives you a primitive value back as the animated value, you can animate nearly any property of a view. But always remember what Uncle Ben said, "With Great Value Comes Great Responsibility". You should always ensure that any animations you use add value and context for your users. Janky, unchoreographed animations feel out of place.

Compared to `ValueAnimator`, however, `ObjectAnimator` is more limited. You can only animate a subset of a view's properties. Here are the properties you can animate for a view:

- **alpha**: Controls the transparency of a view. **0** is a fully transparent, invisible view and **1** is fully opaque.
- **scaleX** and **scaleY**: Control the size and scale of a view on the X and Y axis, respectively.
- **pivotX** and **pivotY**: Control the view's pivot point — the point around which the view rotates. By default, the pivot point is at the center of the view.
- **rotation**, **rotationX**, and **rotationY**: Control the view's rotation in both 2D and 3D.
- **x** and **y**: Control the location of a view on the X and Y axis, respectively.
- **translationX** and **translationY**: Control the location of a view at an offset from its X and Y axis location, respectively.

This chapter closes off with a few challenges to help you practice your newly acquired animation skills. Be sure to try them out.

Challenges

Challenge 1: Animate the title and rating

Earlier in the chapter, you animated the summary of the movie. To take the UX up a notch, animate the title and rating into view as well.

Your challenge is to figure out which animation option works best for this.

Feel free to try a few different property animation types to see what fits best and looks most consistent with the rest of the animations.

The more you play around with these APIs, the better you'll understand how animations work on Android.

Challenge 2: Animate the cast image

As of now, the cast section appears directly into view. It would feel consistent if the cast **faded into** view as well. You could animate the cast list's entire RecyclerView after assigning the cast information to it, but that would feel odd. Instead, you want to animate the cast image after it loads.

To do it correctly, add a new function to `CastViewHolder` and call it right after loading the image drawable into the `castImage` view.

The remaining steps should be relatively straightforward to implement. Pick a property you want to animate and a duration of your choice. Try playing with a few different interpolators to see what feels best in this case. You can also check out the final project to see a possible implementation of it!

In this chapter, you learned the basics of animations and the various options available in Android for animating your views. As you progress through the book, you'll learn even more sophisticated ways of animating different parts of the app.

Key points

- Android offers two ways to animate the properties of your views: `ValueAnimator` and `ObjectAnimator`.
- `ValueAnimator` is a flexible API that lets you take complete control of the animation and animate multiple properties and multiple views at once.
- `ObjectAnimator` lets you animate a single property of one view easily.
- Interpolators let you control the rate of change of the animated property.
- You can change how an animation feels by playing with the duration and interpolator options.

In the next chapter, you'll learn all about adding animations to your custom views.

Chapter 2: Animating Custom Views

By Prateek Prasad

In Chapter 1, "Value & Object Animators", you got an introduction to animations on Android and then wrote your very first view animations. Animating views bundled with the UI toolkit is one of the most common use cases you'll encounter when writing apps; however, it's far from the only one.

While building apps, the regular widgets often feel too limited in what they offer. Building a custom view is a fairly common option for Android developers who are writing custom, highly tailored behaviors. Custom views offer greater control over the view's behavior, while giving you more power to fine-tune the parameters.

In this chapter, you'll look at ways to introduce animations. In the process, you'll also see how to use abstractions to expose only the necessary pieces of the animation control to the custom view consumers.

Setting up the project

Open this chapter's starter project in **Android Studio**. Build and run.

The app is the same as in the last chapter, with one slight modification to the movie details screen.

Tap any movie to open the details screen. Scroll down and add the movie to favorites. You'll notice that, while the operation is in the loading state, a progress bar appears in the button. This custom view, called `FavoriteButton`, is located in the **details** package.

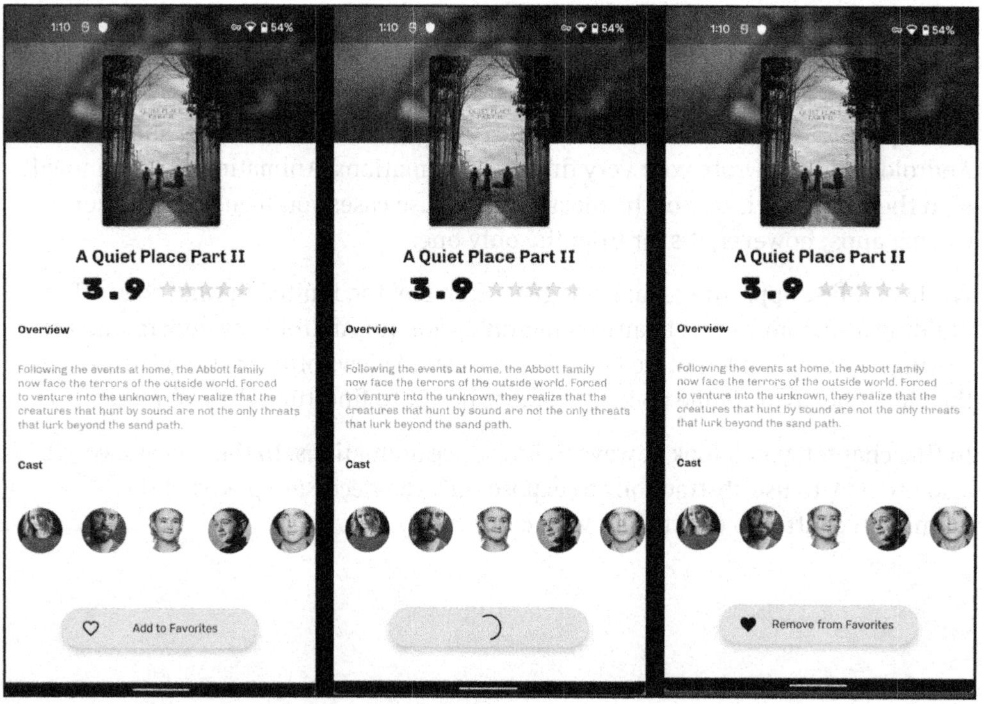

To get a better idea of that final animation, here are frame-by-frame screenshots. If you'd like to see it in action now, build and run the final project for the chapter.

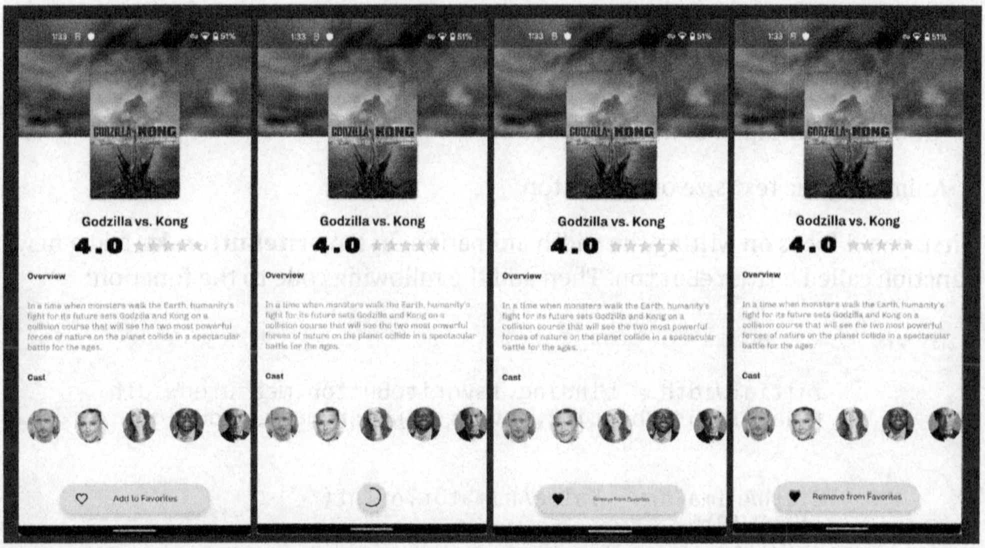

Open **view_favorite_button.xml** from the **res/layout** folder and take a look at the layout for the custom view. Observe that it's comprised of two views, an `ExtendedFloatingActionButton` and a `CircularProgressIndicator`. Now, open **FavoriteButton.kt**. You'll notice that it extends from `ConstraintLayout`. Also notice how `setFavorite` switches the visibility of the progress indicator based on `isFavorite` which is passed from `MovieDetailsFragment`.

The progress indicator appears when `showProgress` is called. Setting the movie's favorite status via `setFavorite` hides it again.

In this chapter, you'll work on adding an animation for this state change. Now that you have your workspace set up, it's time to get your hands dirty!

Building the progress animation

There are three key parts to the progress animation:

- Animating the width of the button.
- Animating the alpha of the progress bar.
- Animating the text size of the button.

First, you'll focus on writing the width animation. In **FavoriteButton.kt**, add a new function called `animateButton`. Then add the following code to the function:

```
private fun animateButton() {
    //1
    val initialWidth = binding.favoriteButton.measuredWidth
    val finalWidth = binding.favoriteButton.measuredHeight

    //2
    val widthAnimator = ValueAnimator.ofInt(
      initialWidth,
      finalWidth
    )

    //3
    widthAnimator.duration = 1000

   //4
    widthAnimator.addUpdateListener {
        binding.favoriteButton.updateLayoutParams {
            this.width = it.animatedValue as Int
        }
    }

    //5
    widthAnimator.start()
}
```

In the code above, you:

1. Set the `initialWidth` to the measured width of the button and the`finalWidth` to the measured height. You want the button to animate from its initial width to a final state where it becomes a circle. To convert a rectangle to a square, you need to make the width and height the same. By that same logic, since the button already has rounded corners, making the width and height the same makes it a circle.
2. Instantiate a `ValueAnimator` using the static `ofInt`, then pass the `intialWidth` and `finalWidth` to it.

3. Assign a 1,000 millisecond duration to the animator.
4. Add an `updateListener` to the animator and assign the `animatedValue` as the width of the button.
5. Finally, you start the animation.

To make the animation run, call the newly created `animateButton` animation from `showProgress` by replacing the `TODO` item.

```
animateButton()
```

Build and run the app. Try tapping on the button. The animation is far from finished and may feel a bit wonky right now, but the width animation should work as expected.

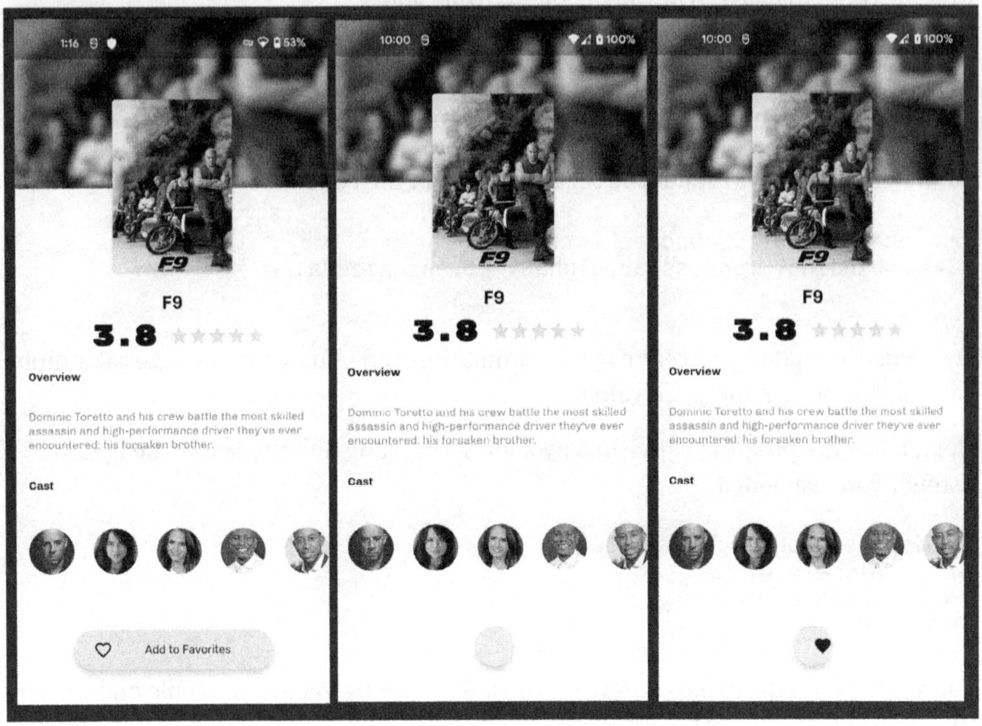

Next, you'll address the **alpha animation** for the progress bar.

Adding the progress bar's alpha animation

Right above the code where you declared `widthAnimator`, add the following code:

```
val alphaAnimator = ObjectAnimator.ofFloat(
  binding.progressBar,
  "alpha",
  0f,
  1f
)
```

You created an `ObjectAnimator` instance using `ofFloat`. You then supplied the property to animate — in this case, `alpha` — along with the start and final values for the animation.

Now, below `widthAnimator.duration = 1000` add:

```
alphaAnimator.duration = 1000
```

You assigned a 1,000 millisecond duration for the animation.

Below `widthAnimator.addUpdateListener`, add the code:

```
alphaAnimator.addUpdateListener {
    binding.progressBar.alpha = it.animatedValue as Float
}
```

You added an `updateListener` for the animation and updated the progressBar alpha value based on the animated value.

Next, make the progress bar visible by adding this code directly below the update listener you just added:

```
binding.progressBar.apply {
    alpha = 0f
    isVisible = true
}
```

You've prepared the `progressBar` for the animation by making it visible and turning its initial alpha down to 0.

Lastly, the following right below `widthAnimator.start()`:

```
alphaAnimator.start()
```

Now you started the animation.

Build and run. Tap **Add to Favorites**. The progress bar now becomes visible as the width change animation takes place.

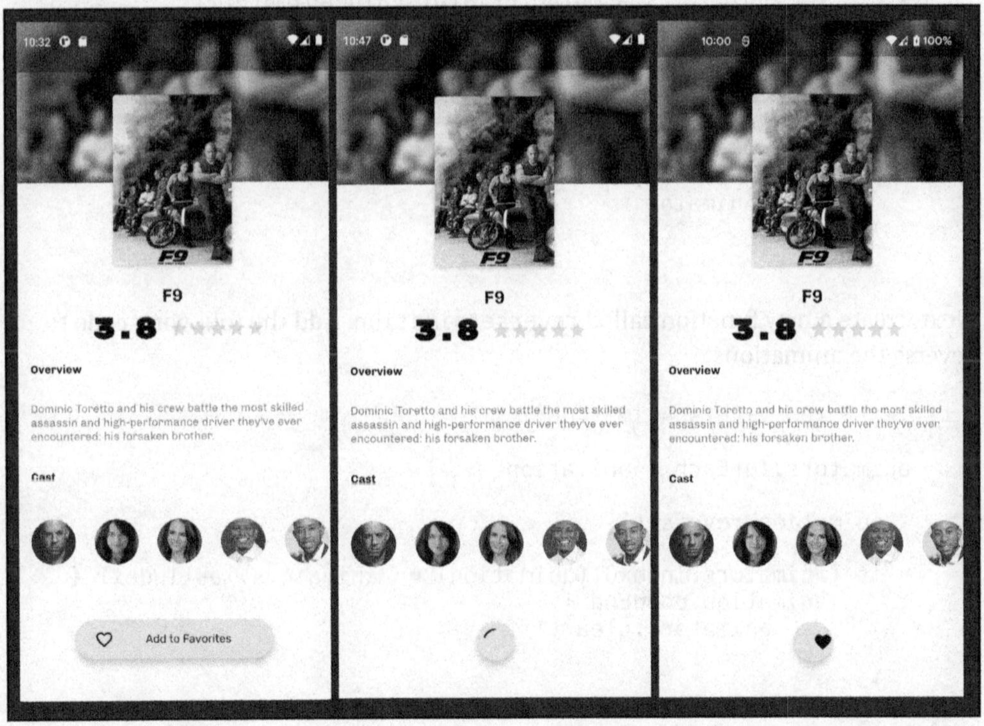

At this point, the animation looks pretty good, but there's an elephant in the room: While the animation starts as expected, the app ends up in a broken state once the animation completes.

You'll fix that next.

Reversing the animations

To fix the button's behavior, you need to make it go back to its initial state after the animation completes. In other words, you need to reverse the animation. Luckily for you, the animation APIs on Android make this pretty straightforward.

To reverse the animation, you need to maintain a reference of all the animators you created.

Right above the `init{}` block in **FavoriteButton.kt**, add the following code:

```
private val animators = mutableListOf<ValueAnimator>()
```

Now, right before you start the animators in `animateButton`, add the following:

```
animators.addAll(
    listOf(
        widthAnimator,
        alphaAnimator
    )
)
```

Next, create a new function called `reverseAnimation`. Add the following code to reverse the animations:

```
private fun reverseAnimation() {
  //1
  animators.forEach { animation ->
    //2
    animation.reverse()
    //3
    if (animators.indexOf(animation) == animators.lastIndex) {
        animation.doOnEnd {
            animators.clear()
        }
    }
  }
}
```

To unpack what's going on here:

1. You loop over the animations list one by one.
2. Then, you call `reverse` on each animation. Yep! It's that easy, just a single function call.
3. Once all the animations are reversed, you clear out the list to keep it tidy and to avoid adding duplicate references to it the next time the animation triggers.

All that's left is to call `reverseAnimation`. Do that from `hideProgress` by replacing the `TODO` item.

```
reverseAnimation()
```

All right, it's time for the big reveal. Build and run. Tap **Add to Favorites** to trigger the animation. It looks pretty sweet, doesn't it?

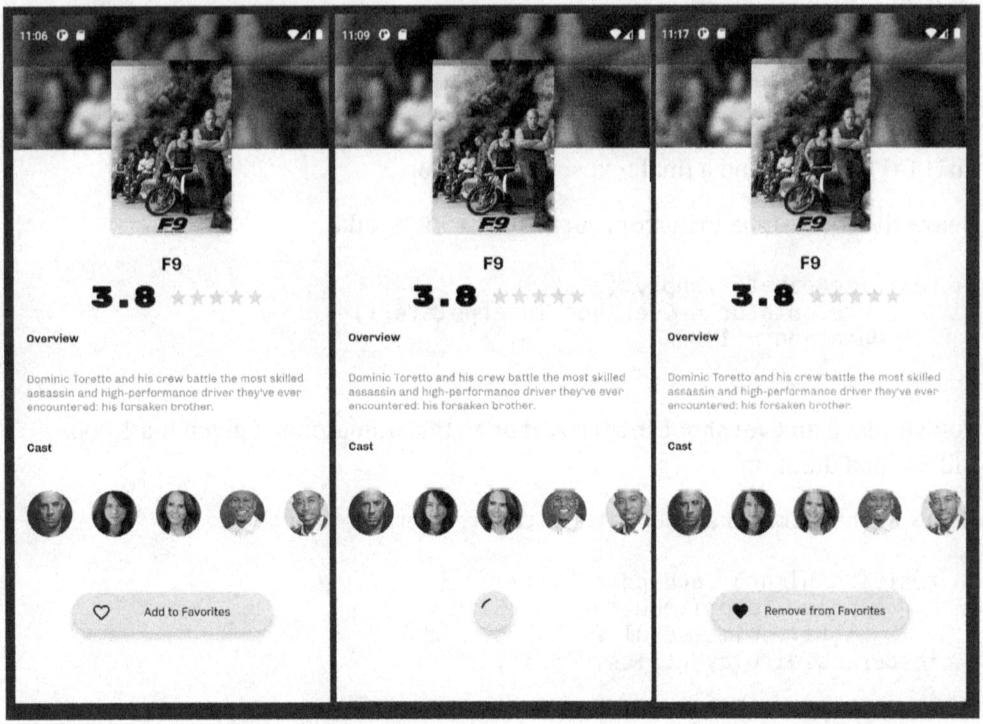

There's a slightly rough edge here that would be great to polish out: When the text comes back into view, it feels very choppy!

As a final step, you'll add a subtle animation to tie everything together.

Animating the text size

To animate the text size, add the code below at the top of `animateButton` just below the declaration for `finalWidth`:

```
val initialTextSize = binding.favoriteButton.textSize
```

This assigned the `initialTextSize` to the button's current text size.

Next, add the new ValueAnimator right below the declaration for alphaAnimator:

```
val textSizeAnimator = ValueAnimator.ofFloat(
  initialTextSize,
  0f
)
```

You just created a ValueAnimator using the static ofFloat, then passed it the initialTextSize and a final text size value of 0.

Below the code alphaAnimator.duration = 1000, add:

```
textSizeAnimator.apply {
    interpolator = OvershootInterpolator()
    duration = 1000
}
```

You've added an OvershootInterpolator to the animator and given it a 1,000 millisecond duration.

Below alphaAnimator.addUpdateListener, insert the code:

```
textSizeAnimator.addUpdateListener {
    binding.favoriteButton.textSize =
        (it.animatedValue as Float) /
resources.displayMetrics.density
}
```

This code assigned an updateListener to the animator and updated the text size of the button using animatedValue. Since the text size needs to be an sp value, you have to divide the animated value by the screen density.

Right below alphaAnimator.start(), add:

```
textSizeAnimator.start()
```

This will start the animation.

As a final step, add the `textSizeAnimator` to the `animators` list.

```
animators.addAll(
    listOf(
        widthAnimator,
        alphaAnimator,
        textSizeAnimator
    )
)
```

Finally, build and run. You'll notice a considerable difference in the feel of the animation.

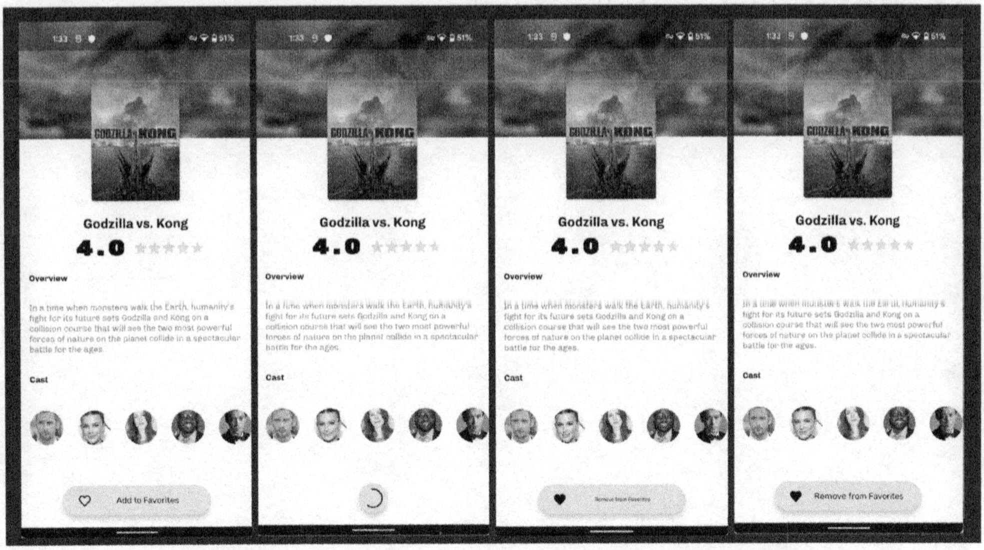

This cleanup will make it easier for you (and others) to scan this function and quickly understand what's going on.

You did a great job with the animation in this chapter! Even though it might seem like you just worked on a single button and its animation, this was an essential exercise on how to animate the different elements of a custom view, one step at a time.

Key points

- It's easier to work with complex animation when you break them down into smaller individual animations.
- You can reverse animations by calling the **reverse()** function.
- You can create different value animations for different components of a custom view.
- When creating a value animator on text size it needs to be an `sp` value, so you can divide the animated value by the screen density.
- A custom view's animations can be fine tuned and abstracted away from the custom view's consumer, keeping the code simple and the animations concise.

Chapter 3: XML Animations

By Prateek Prasad

In the last two chapters, you learned about animation basics, including two of the most common ways of writing animations on Android, `ValueAnimator` and `ObjectAnimator`. However, you have multiple ways to write animations in Android. Before wrapping up the first section of the book, you'll look at another handy way to create animations for views on Android: XML.

Why use XML animations?

In Chapter 1, "Value & Object Animators" and Chapter 2, "Animating Custom Views", you created animations purely in code. In the current chapter, you will replicate the same animations in XML. While having multiple options to create animations gives you more flexibility, it's vital to understand the significance of XML animations so you can make informed decisions when deciding which option to use.

Writing animations in XML makes your animation code reusable. You only need to declare the core animation once, then use it for any view you want.

To bring consistency to the UX of your app, you want similar components to behave in a similar, consistent manner across screens. Declaring animation behaviors once in XML makes achieving this consistency easy.

Another great advantage of XML-based animations is the ability to swap out your animations with minimal effort. You only need to change the XML declaration instead of changing every instance of the animation implementation written in code.

That said, XML-based animations aren't a silver bullet. For one-off standalone animations, XML-based animations are a lot of work. In such scenarios, writing animations in code takes significantly less time.

With these insights, you can make more informed decisions about which implementation to choose.

Setting up the project

Open this chapter's starter project in Android Studio. Build and run.

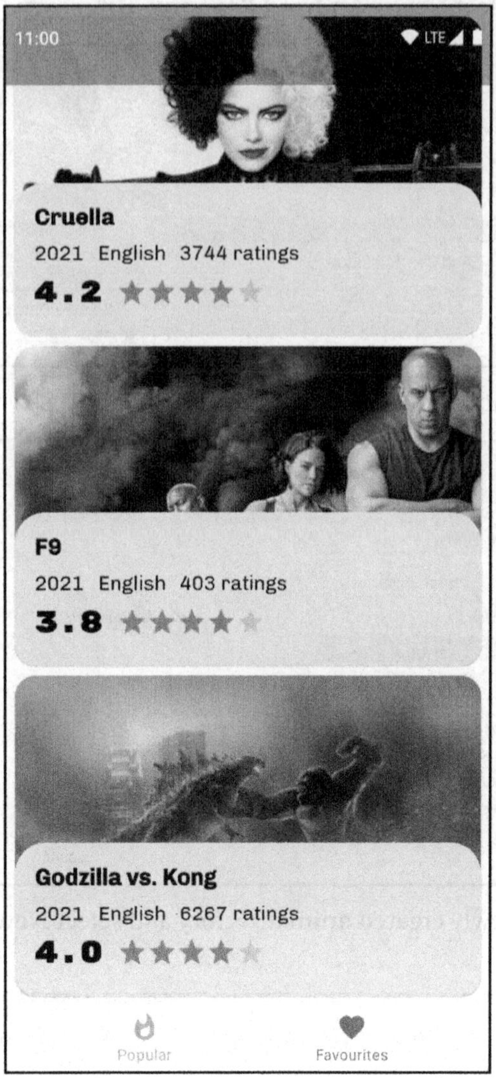

It's the same project you've worked on in previous chapters, but the animations have been stripped out. In this chapter, you'll recreate the animations you added to the details screen in the first chapter using XML instead of Kotlin.

Writing your first view animation in XML

To kick things off, you'll animate the backdrop in the details screen. Right-click on the **res** folder and select **New ▸ Android Resource Directory**.

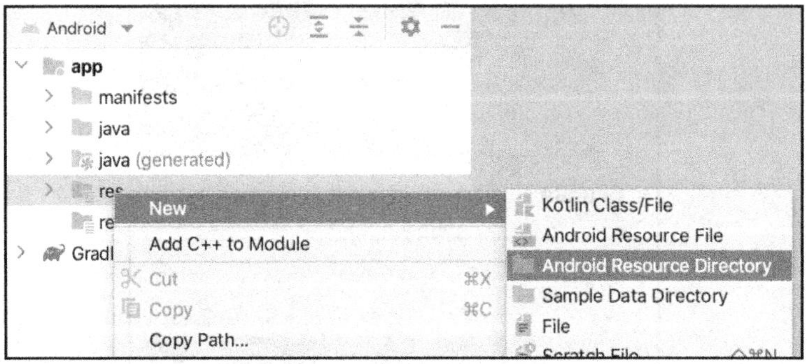

Next, create a new directory named **anim**.

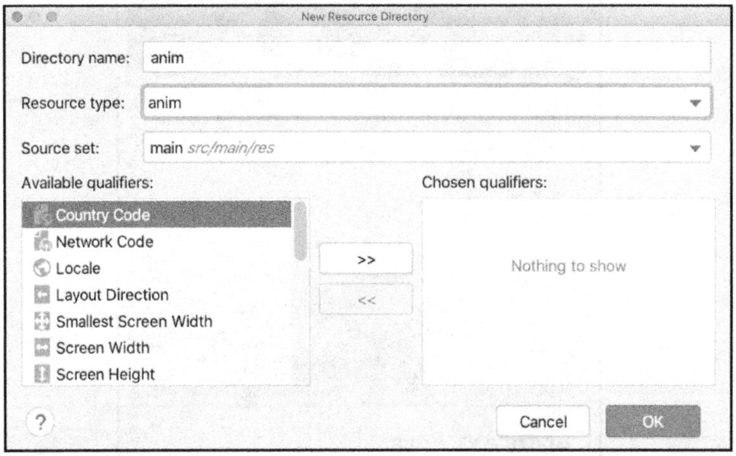

Right-click on the newly created **anim** directory and select **New ▸ Animation Resource File**.

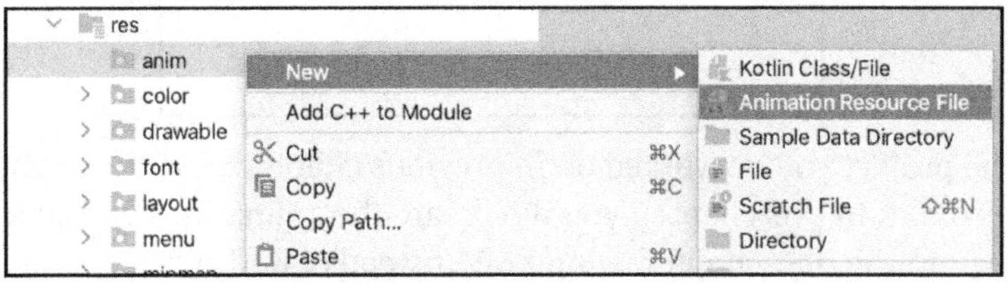

Finally, name the XML file **backdrop_animation**. Good job. You've now created the file where you'll write the definition for the backdrop's animation.

Start by adding the following to **backdrop_animation.xml**:

```
<?xml version="1.0" encoding="utf-8"?>
<translate
  xmlns:android="http://schemas.android.com/apk/res/android"
  android:duration="1000"
  android:fromYDelta="20%"
  android:toYDelta="0%"
  android:interpolator="@android:interpolator/
decelerate_cubic" />
```

The animation instructions in this XML determine the transformations that will occur. Here's a breakdown of what's going on in the snippet above:

- **translate**: Defines which kind of transformation this animation will use. When you define view animations in XML, the file must contain a single root tag, which can be an `<alpha>`, `<scale>`, `<translate>`, `<rotate>`, interpolator element or a `<set>` element that holds groups of these elements.
- **android:duration**: The duration of the animation in milliseconds. The duration will be `1000` which is equal to one second.
- **android:fromYDelta**: The start position of the view on the y-axis. In this case, it has an offset of **20%** from its original position.
- **android:toYDelta**: The end position of the view on the y-axis. In this case, you want the view to go back to its original position, so it should have an offset of **0%**.
- **android:interpolator**: The interpolator to use for this animation. In this case, it's the **decelerate interpolator**.

Now that you've defined the animation semantics, it's time to plug in the information and make it play.

Playing the animation

Open **MovieDetailsFragment.kt** and replace the `//TODO` in `animateBackdrop()` with the following:

```
//1
val animation = AnimationUtils.loadAnimation(
  requireContext(),
  R.anim.backdrop_animation
)
//2
binding.backdrop.startAnimation(animation)
```

Here's what's happening:

1. Loads the animation file using `AnimationUtils.loadAnimation()`.
2. Starts the animation on the `backdrop`.

Build and run. You'll see the backdrop slide into place.

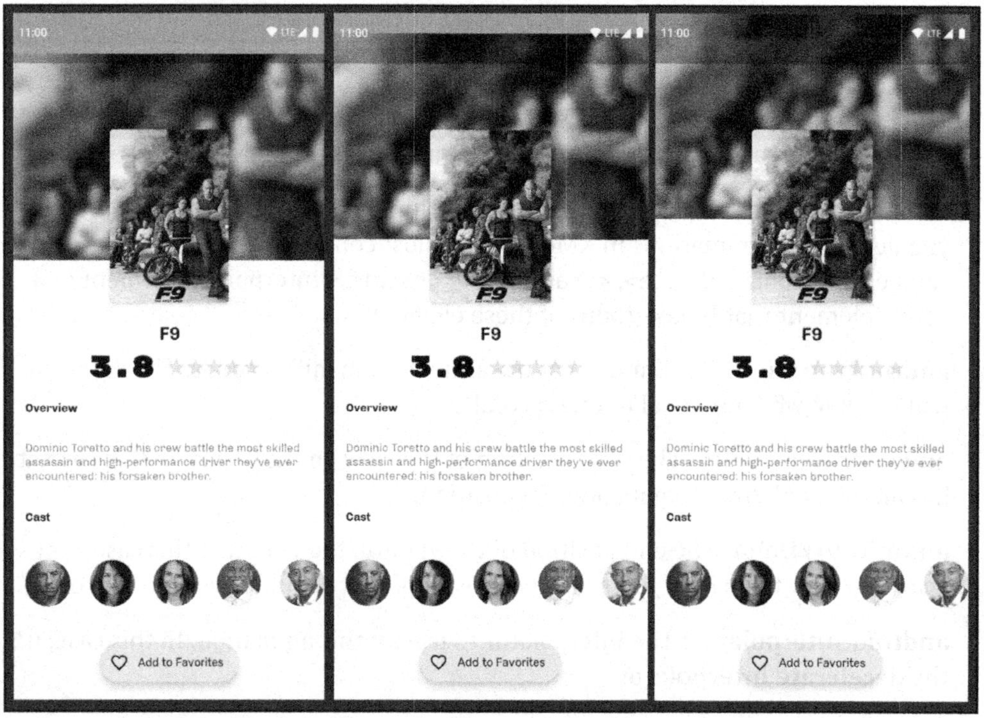

If you compare this method of creating the animation to what you did in the first chapter, you'll notice that you needed to write far less code here.

Learning the caveats of the view animation

While view animations are relatively straightforward to work with and feel quite flexible, Google recommends against using them, in part because their final behavior can be deceptive.

Consider the translate animation you wrote above, and assume you wrote it for a button. For now, it works as you expect it to *visually*:

It translates the view from an offset to its final position.

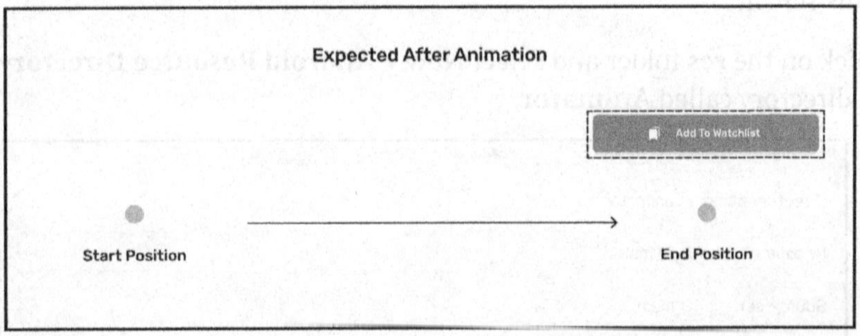

However, instead of moving the actual view, it only translates its pixels — that is, its bitmap.

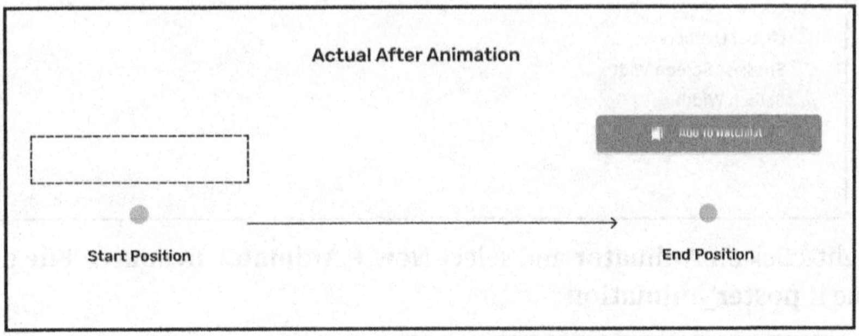

Notice that the button is no longer clickable after the animation finishes because, while the button's bitmap moved to the final position, the button still exists at the start position. This is deceptive about view animations. A view animation works great for our background, but would not be a good choice for other elements in the layout like buttons.

Now that you've seen the most basic type of animation in Android and learned about its limitations, it's time to take a look at more modern alternatives. Next you'll learn about the **Animator API**, which includes derived classes **ValueAnimator** and **ObjectAnimator**.

Using ValueAnimator in XML

As the next step, you'll use the **ValueAnimator API** in XML to animate the poster in the details screen.

Right-click on the **res** folder and select **New ▸ Android Resource Directory** and create a directory called **Animator**.

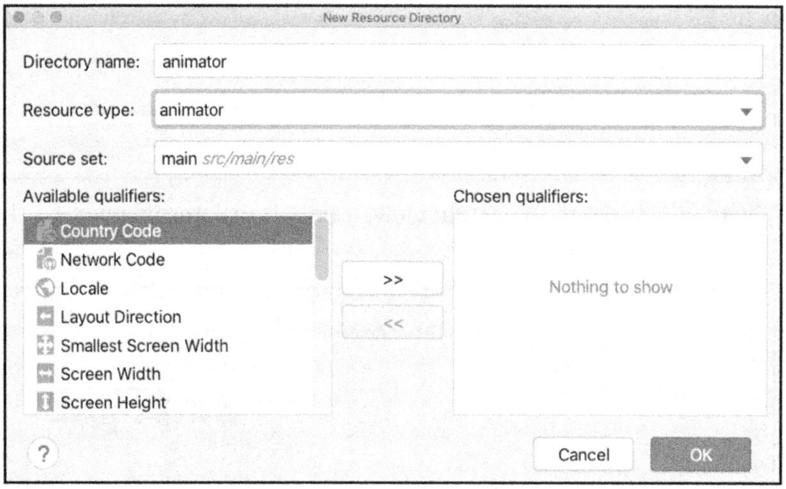

Then, right-click on **Animator** and select **New ▸ Animator Resource File** directory and name it **poster_animation**:

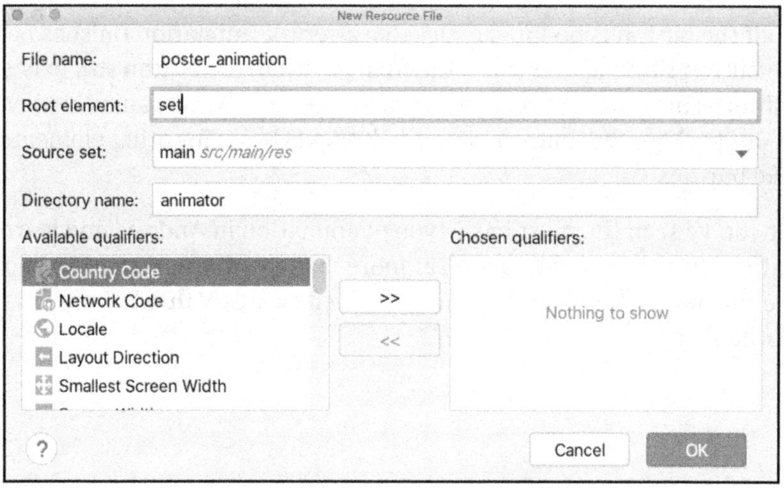

Replace the existing code in the file with:

```
<?xml version="1.0" encoding="utf-8"?>
<animator
    xmlns:android="http://schemas.android.com/apk/res/android"
    android:duration="1000"
    android:interpolator="@android:interpolator/overshoot"
    android:valueFrom="0.0"
    android:valueTo="1.0"
    android:valueType="floatType" />
```

Here's what you need to know about the snippet above:

- **animator**: Declares a `ValueAnimator` in XML.
- **android:duration**: The duration of the animation.
- **android:interpolator**: The interpolator for this animation. In this case, you're using the overshoot interpolator.
- **android:valueFrom**: The starting value of the animation.
- **android:valueTo**: The end value of the animation.
- **android:valueType**: The value type, which can be either `floatType` or `intType`.

Now that you've defined `ValueAnimator`, it's time to use it. Open **MovieDetailsFragment.kt** and replace the `//TODO` in `animatePoster()` with the following code:

```
//1
val animation =
  AnimatorInflater.loadAnimator(
    requireContext(),
    R.animator.poster_animation
  ) as ValueAnimator

animation.apply {
  //2
  addUpdateListener { animation ->
    val animatedValue = animation.animatedValue as Float
    binding.posterContainer.alpha = animatedValue
    binding.posterContainer.scaleX = animatedValue
    binding.posterContainer.scaleY = animatedValue
  }
  //3
  start()
}
```

Here's what this code does:

1. Loads the animation using `AnimatorInflater.loadAnimator()`, then casts it to a `ValueAnimator`. `loadAnimator()` returns an `Animator` object which is why the cast is needed.
2. Adds `updateListener` to the animator and updates the `alpha`, `scaleX` and `scaleY` properties.
3. Starts the animation.

Build and run. The poster now scales up and fades into place when you launch the details screen.

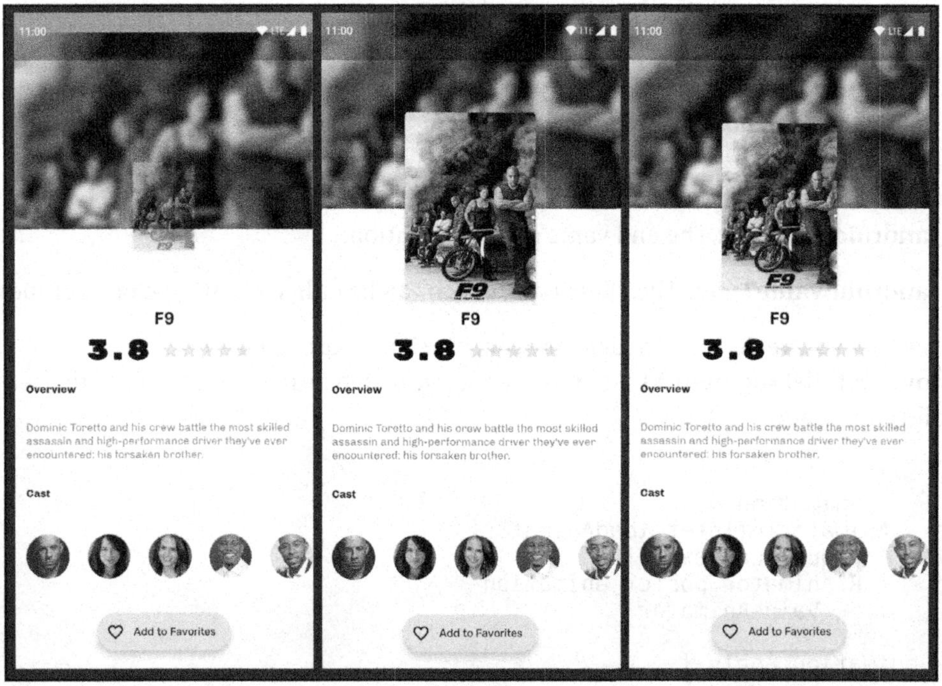

So far in this chapter, you've created two resource directories, the **anim** and the **animator** directories. Here's how the two differ:

- **animator**: Stores the XML files that define the property animation declarations: `ValueAnimators` and `ObjectAnimators`.
- **anim**: Stores the XML files that define the view animation declarations and tween animation declarations. You can also store property animation declarations here, but it's better to store them separately in the **animator** directory so that the code is more organized and it's easy to tell the difference between the two.

Using ObjectAnimator in XML

Next, you'll animate the movie summary text. This time, you'll leverage `ObjectAnimator` via XML to achieve the effect.

Create a new file in the **animator** directory and name it **text_animation**. Then, replace the existing code in the file with:

```
<?xml version="1.0" encoding="utf-8"?>
<objectAnimator
    xmlns:android="http://schemas.android.com/apk/res/android"
    android:duration="1000"
    android:propertyName="alpha"
    android:valueFrom="0.0"
    android:valueTo="1.0"
    android:valueType="floatType" />
```

Here are the important parts of the code above:

- **objectAnimator**: Declares an `ObjectAnimator` in XML.
- **android:duration**: The duration of the animation.
- **android:propertyName**: The name of the property you're animating.
- **android:valueFrom**: The starting value of the animation.
- **android:valueTo**: The end value of the animation.
- **android:valueType**: A value type that can be either `floatType` or `intType`.

Now that you've defined `ObjectAnimator`, it's time to plug it in. Open **MovieDetailsFragment.kt** and replace the `//TODO` in the `animateText()` function with the following:

```
//1
val textAnimation = AnimatorInflater.loadAnimator(
  requireContext(),
  R.animator.text_animation
) as ObjectAnimator
//2
textAnimation.target = binding.summary
//3
textAnimation.start()
```

Here's the breakdown of the snippet:

1. Loads the animation using `AnimatorInflater.loadAnimator()`.
2. Sets the summary TextView as the target for the animation.
3. Starts the animator.

Build and run. You'll now see the summary text fade in when you launch the details screen.

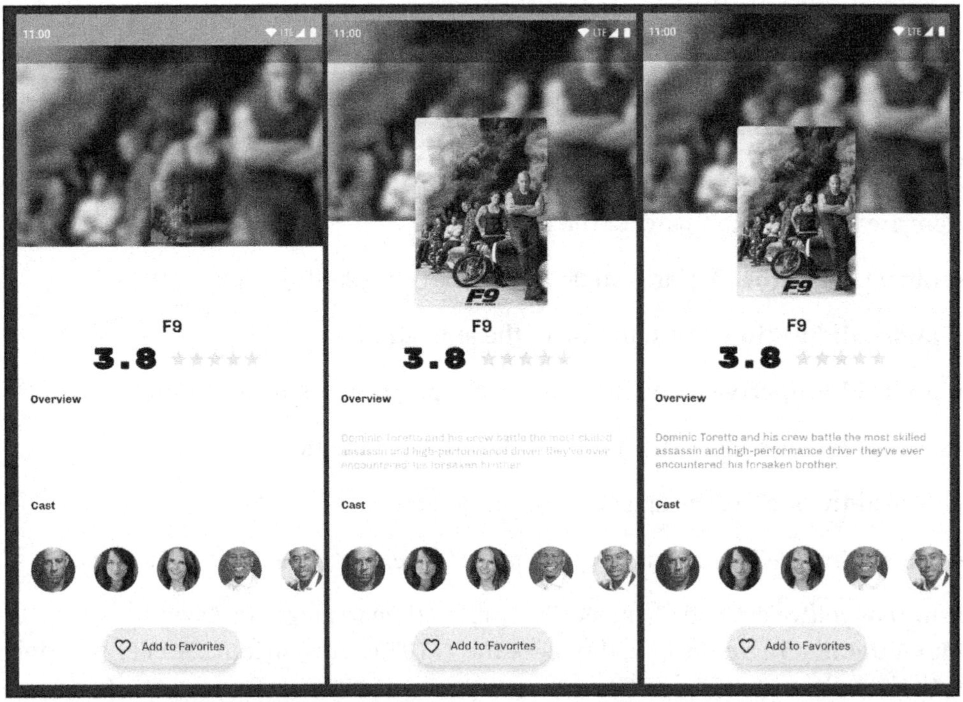

So far, you've animated single properties, but you might run into situations where you need to animate multiple properties of a view at once. That's what you'll work on next.

Chaining multiple animations together

To chain multiple animations, you'll use the `AnimatorSet` API. `AnimatorSet` lets you chain multiple animations and play them either in sequence or at once.

Right now, the poster image uses an animated value from `ValueAnimator` to animate the scale and alpha properties. You'll switch its implementation to an AnimatorSet instead.

Create a new XML file in the animator directory and name it **poster_animator_set**. Then, add the following code to the file:

```
<?xml version="1.0" encoding="utf-8"?>
<!-- 1 -->
<set xmlns:android="http://schemas.android.com/apk/res/android"
    android:ordering="together">

    <!-- 2 -->
    <objectAnimator
        android:duration="1000"
        android:interpolator="@android:interpolator/overshoot"
        android:propertyName="alpha"
        android:valueFrom="0f"
        android:valueTo="1f" />

    <!-- 3 -->
    <objectAnimator
        android:duration="1000"
        android:interpolator="@android:interpolator/overshoot"
        android:propertyName="scaleX"
        android:valueFrom="0"
        android:valueTo="1"
        android:valueType="floatType" />
    <!-- 4 -->
    <objectAnimator
        android:duration="1000"
        android:interpolator="@android:interpolator/overshoot"
        android:propertyName="scaleY"
        android:valueFrom="0"
        android:valueTo="1"
        android:valueType="floatType" />
</set>
```

Here's what's happening:

1. You use `set` to declare an animator set. `android:ordering` specifies the order in which the animator set's children will play. In this case, they'll play at the same time, or `together`.
2. The first `objectAnimator` animates the **alpha** property from **0** to **1**.
3. The second `objectAnimator` animates the **scaleX** property from **0** to **1**.
4. The third `objectAnimator` animates the **scaleY** property from **0** to **1**.All three `objectAnimators` run for **1,000** milliseconds and use the **overshoot interpolator**.

Now that you've defined your animator set, it's time to use it. Open **MovieDetailsFragment.kt** and replace the code in `animatePoster()` with the following:

```
//1
val animation = AnimatorInflater.loadAnimator(
  requireContext(),
  R.animator.poster_animator_set
) as AnimatorSet

//2
animation.apply {
  setTarget(binding.posterContainer)
  start()
}
```

The snippet you just added:

1. Loads the animator using `AnimatorInflater.loadAnimator()` and casts it to an `AnimatorSet`.
2. Sets the `posterContainer` view as the target for the `AnimatorSet` and starts the animation.

Build and run. The poster should animate just like before, but with a new implementation under the hood.

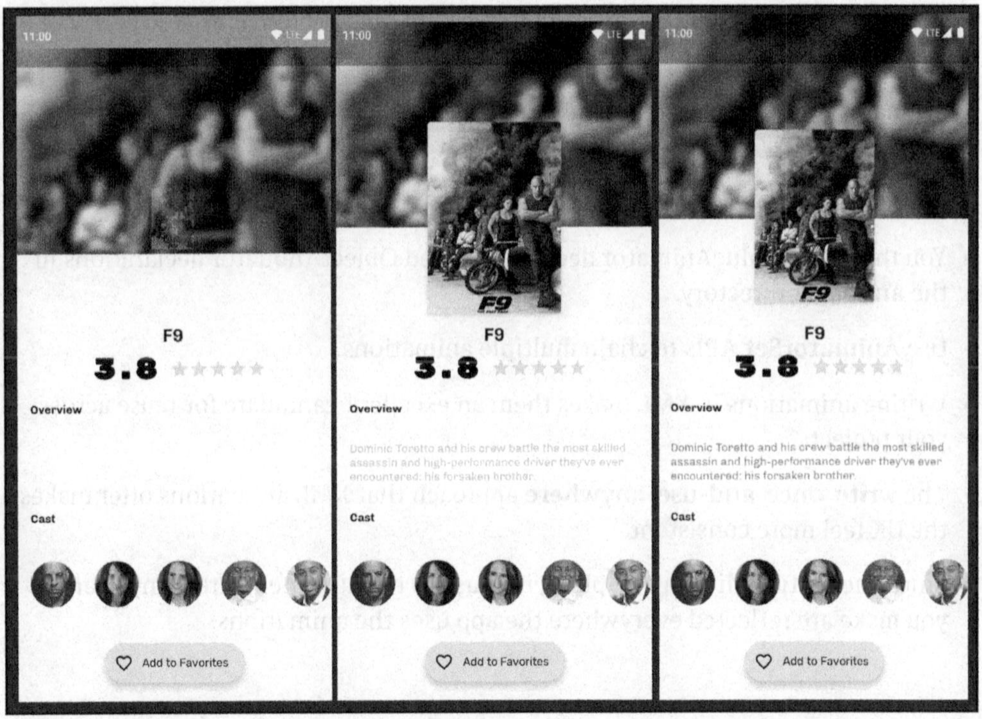

You've done a great job recreating the animations so far. They look fantastic!

Now that you've wrapped up this chapter and the book's first section, you know how to animate individual views and their corresponding properties. In the upcoming section, you'll learn about transitions and how to animate entering and exiting a screen.

Key points

- Working with View animations can often create unexpected or broken behavior in your UI.
- Animator APIs are a safer and more modern alternative to View Animations.
- You store tween animation declarations and View animation declarations in the **anim** directory
- You then store ValueAnimator declarations and ObjectAnimator declarations in the **animator** directory.
- Use **AnimatorSet** APIs to chain multiple animations.
- Writing animations in XML makes them an excellent candidate for reuse across your project.
- The **write-once-and-use-anywhere** approach that XML animations offer makes the UX feel more consistent.
- Since declarations live in one place, it's easy to refactor them later. Any changes you make are reflected everywhere the app uses the animations.

Section II: Screen Transitions

In this section, you'll learn about one of the most important types of animations found in an app, transitions. Screen transitions help your user understand where they are at when moving from one activity or fragment to another. You'll begin by animating transitions with XML animations. You'll create complex transitions between activities and fragments utilizing animation sets. You'll apply animations to specific views during a transition using the Transition Framework. This will allow you to make even more complex and intriguing transitions between fragments and activities. You'll also get a primer on how to troubleshoot some of the most common pitfalls you'll run into when utilizig the transition framework.

Lastly, and most exciting, you'll learn about Element Transitions. This allows a transition to center the focus around a shared element between two fragments and does not require transitioning the whole view heirarcy. Instead, the shared element takes the center stage and becomes a powerful visual effect. You'll learn how to do a circular reveal to reveal tab content, and how to use custom transitions to make the transition attractive.

Chapter 4: Animating Activity & Fragment Transitions With XML

By Alex Sullivan

The transition between screens is one of the most essential types of animation you can add to an app. Screen transitions add continuity as your user moves between different activities. They allow users to get a sense of where they are in your app and where the previous screen's content went. All this makes screen transitions a fundamental part of a polished, enjoyable app.

In this chapter, you'll:

- Use XML **ANIM** files to animate between the authorization and main activities.
- Learn about the different types of navigation component fragment animations.
- Add complex transitions between screens using animation sets.

First, you'll learn about how to animate transitions between activities.

Transitioning between activities

Activities are fundamental building blocks of Android apps. An activity provides a window where the app can draw its UI. Typically, an activity will fill the entire screen, and each activity implements one screen in the app. While many newer Android apps are moving towards a single activity architecture, chances are you'll work on apps with multiple activities, too, so you need to know how to create animations between them.

You can use two methods to animate between activities:

1. **ANIM** resource files
2. The **Transition** framework

In this chapter, you'll focus on the first option: creating activity animations with **ANIM** resource files. While the Transition framework is a more modern and flexible way to create animations, old-fashioned ANIM resource files still drive most animations because they're so simple. You'll learn how to use the Transition framework for fragment animations in the next chapter.

Now, it's time to see how activity animations work.

Components of an activity animation

Activity transitions have two core components:

1. The ANIM resource file that drives the animation.
2. The call to `overridePendingTransition`, which sets the animation on the activity.

You use the ANIM resource file to define the actual animation you want to run on the screen. Animation primitives like `alpha`, `scale` and `translate` define how the animation should look.

Finally, you supply those ANIM resource files to `overridePendingTransition`, which sets up the animation to run when you transition to another activity.

To see this in action, look at the method header for `overridePendingTransition`:

```
public void overridePendingTransition(int enterAnim, int
exitAnim)
```

`overridePendingTransition` is a method in `Activity` that allows you to specify a resource for the enter and exit animations. You'll typically call `overridePendingTransition` **after** a call to `startActivity`. The `enterAnim` resource describes the animation for the **incoming** animation. Conversely, the `exitAnim` resource describes the animation for the **outgoing** activity.

If you want to trigger a specific animation while finishing an `Activity`, use `overridePendingTransition` **after** a call to `finish`. In that scenario, `exitAnim` will describe the animation of the `Activity` when it finishes, while `enterAnim` will describe the animation of the `Activity` when it resumes.

> **Note**: Since `overridePendingTransition` is a method in `Activity`, its challenging to use when you're specifying an animation from a component outside of your `Activity`. In that case, use `ActivityOptions.makeCustomAnimation` to create a `Bundle` and pass it to `startActivity`. It takes the same enter and exit animations and works the same way as `overridePendingTransition`.

Now that you understand how activity transitions work, it's time to see how to use them in your own apps.

Getting started

Open the starter project within **04-activity-transitions** in the **aat-materials** repository, using Android Studio Arctic Fox or newer.

Once the project syncs, build and run the app the tap the **Sign In** button. You'll see the login screen.

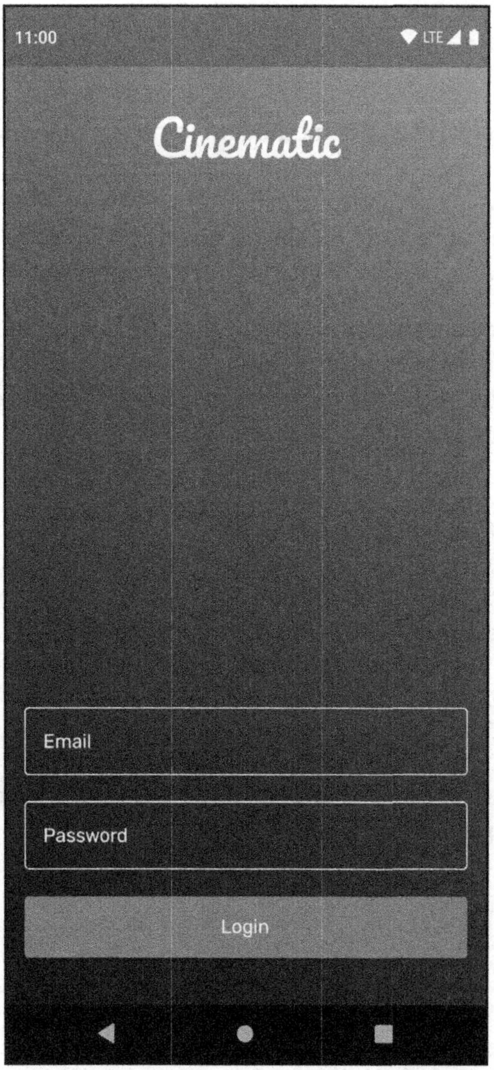

You'll create a fancy animation to go between `AuthActivity`, where the user enters their login and signup credentials, and `MainActivity`, where the movie list lives.

You want to animate `AuthActivity` to fade into the background while `MainActivity` slides in. To emphasize that `AuthActivity` is leaving the screen, you'll scale it down in size, move it lower on the screen and make it slowly fade away. `MainActivity` will slide up and fade in while `AuthActivity` disappears.

Here's how the animations will look:

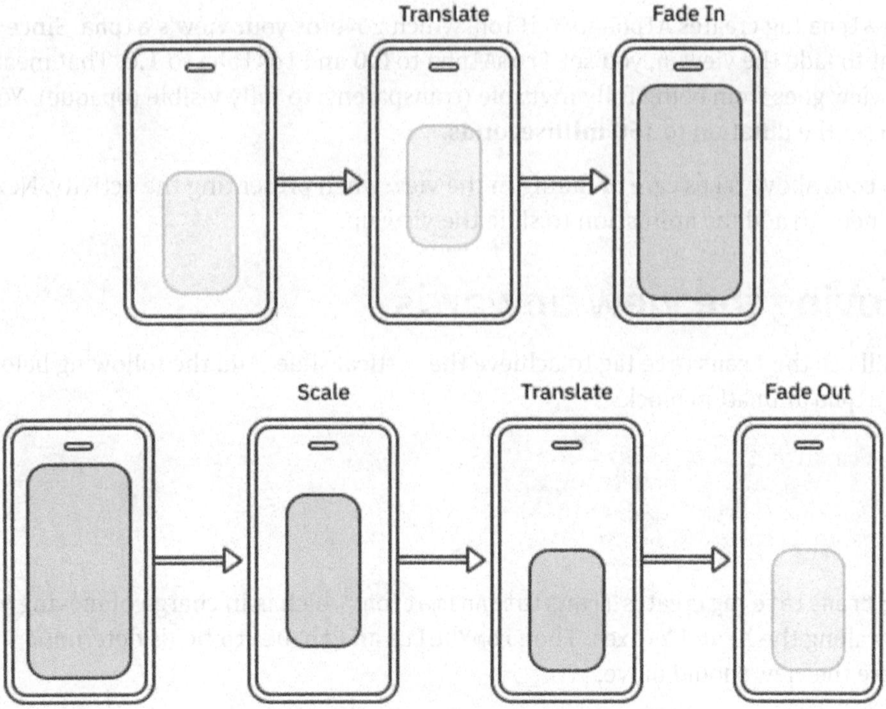

Creating the activity enter animation

You'll start building the `AuthActivity` to `MainActivity` animation by focusing on the **enter animation**, which runs on the `MainActivity` UI as it comes into view.

First, open the ANIM resource file named **auth_main_enter** in the **anim** resource directory. You need to store the file in the **anim** resource directory because the activity animations API relies on the older, tween-style animations, rather than the newer animator animations.

Right now, the file has an empty `set` tag that defines `AnimationSet`, which contains a set of animations. You want your enter transition to include both moving the activity up *and* fading it in, so your `set` needs to contain both of those animations.

To start, create an `alpha` animation in the body of the `set` tag:

```
<alpha
  android:duration="150"
  android:fromAlpha="0.0"
  android:toAlpha="1.0" />
```

The `alpha` tag creates `AlphaAnimation`, which governs your view's `alpha`. Since you want to fade the view *in*, you set `fromAlpha` to **0.0** and `toAlpha` to **1.0**. That means the view goes from being fully invisible (transparent) to fully visible (opaque). You also set the duration to **150 milliseconds**.

The code above takes care of fading in the view when presenting the activity. Next, you need to add the animation to slide the view up.

Moving the view upwards

You'll use the `translate` tag to achieve the vertical slide. Add the following below the `alpha` animation block:

```
<translate
  android:duration="300"
  android:fromYDelta="100%p"
  android:toYDelta="0" />
```

The `translate` tag creates `TranslateAnimation`, which is in charge of moving your view along the X- and Y- axes. The `fromYDelta` and `toYDelta` fields determine where the view should move.

In this case, you instruct the translation animation to move the view from a Y-delta of **100%** of the screen size to a Y-delta of **0**. 0 represents the top of the screen, so you're moving the view from the bottom of the screen up to the top. That is, the view is sliding up from the bottom.

The `translate` animation can also translate X coordinates using the `fromXDelta` and `toXDelta` fields.

Note: In the example above, you use a percentage value in `fromYDelta`. You could also use a raw pixel count by hardcoding a number. To translate from a Y-delta of 20 pixels to a Y-delta of 5 pixels, you'd just hardcode the numbers 20 and 5 without a percent sign.

At this point, you've finished the activity enter transition. Now, it's time to work on the more complex exit transition.

Creating the activity exit transition

Now that you've created the enter animation, it's time to build the exit animation to govern how `AuthActivity` leaves the screen when transitioning to `MainActivity`.

Start by opening the ANIM resource file in the **anim** resource directory named **auth_main_exit**. Just as you did with **auth_main_enter**, you'll add animations to the empty `set` inside.

For a refresher, the goal of the exit animation is to scale the view to a smaller size while also translating the view down and fading it out.

Start by adding the `alpha` animation to the body of the set. This will fade the view out:

```
<alpha
  android:duration="@android:integer/config_mediumAnimTime"
  android:fromAlpha="1.0"
  android:toAlpha="0.0" />
```

This time, you change from an alpha value of **1** to an alpha value of **0**, which fades the view out. You also use one of the default animation time durations included in the Android SDK.

Next, add the translation to move the view down:

```
<translate
  android:duration="@android:integer/config_mediumAnimTime"
  android:fromYDelta="0.0"
  android:toYDelta="20.0%p" />
```

This time, you translate the view from a starting position at the top of the screen down by **20%** of the screen height. You slide down by 20% instead of 100% because you want the downward slide to be subtle.

Building the scale animation

Now that you've handled fading the view out and sliding it down, it's time to add the scale animation. Start by adding the following below the `translate` block:

```
<scale
  android:duration="@android:integer/config_shortAnimTime"
  android:fromXScale="1.0"
  android:fromYScale="1.0"
  android:toXScale="0.9"
  android:toYScale="0.9"
  android:pivotX="50%p"
  android:pivotY="50%p" />
```

Here's a breakdown of what's going on:

- The **scale** animation scales a view up or down on both the X- and Y-axes. Here, you're saying the animation should start from a scale of **1.0**, the normal scaling for the view.
- **toXScale** and **toYScale** indicate what the final scaling should be. You used a value of **0.9** here, meaning that the final scaled-down view should be 90% of the size of the original view. It might not seem like much, but subtlety is important in animation.
- Finally, **pivotX** and **pivotY** indicate the center of the scale animation. In other words, it's the point the view should scale *toward*. Using **50%** indicates that the view should scale toward the center of the view.

Now that you've defined the enter and exit animations, you can wire them up and see the activity transition in action.

Wiring up the enter and exit activity transitions

Open **AuthActivity.kt** and navigate to the call to `startActivity` in `onCreate`. Add the following below the call to `startActivity`:

```
overridePendingTransition(R.anim.auth_main_enter,
R.anim.auth_main_exit)
```

Here, you set the enter and exit animations for the activity using the animation files you fleshed out earlier.

Build and run the app. Tap the **Sign In** button, then the **Log In** button to progress to the main activity. You'll see the authorization activity scale down and fadeaway, while the main activity slides up and fades in.

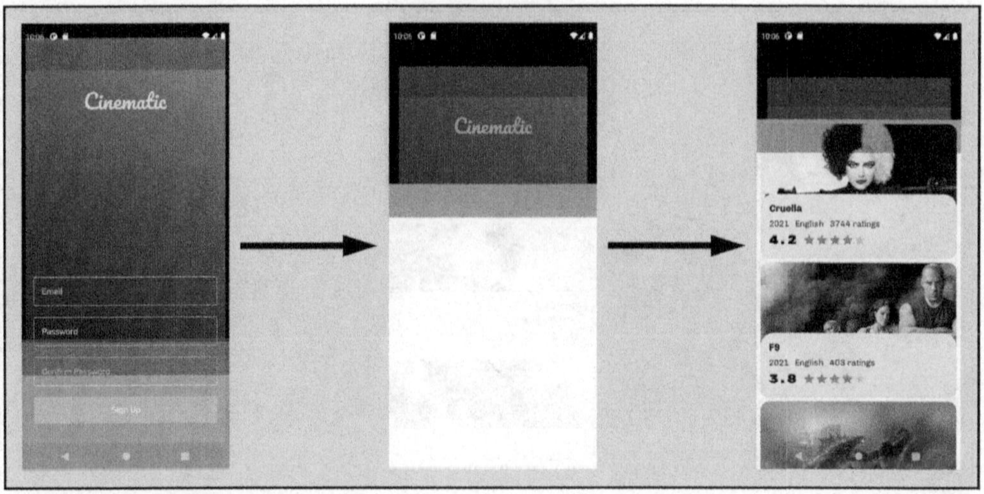

The animation looks good, but a couple of things stand out:

1. The exit animation gets lost in the background when the enter animation slides up. Ideally, you'd delay the enter animation until the exit animation finishes playing.
2. The animation is too linear. The enter animation slides up without any easing, which makes it feel mechanical and unnatural.

Next, you'll solve both of these issues.

Polishing the activity transitions

Your first step is to delay the enter animation to give the exit animation more time to shine.

Open **auth_main_enter.xml** file. Add the following line to the `set` declaration at the top of the file:

```
android:startOffset="200"
```

`startOffset` delays the start of the animation by the amount of time you specify. In this scenario, you set an offset of **200 milliseconds** to give the exit animation a bit more time to shine.

Build and run the app again. Navigate back to the main screen to trigger the animation. Now, the exit animation runs long enough to be fully emphasized before the enter transition starts. Much better!

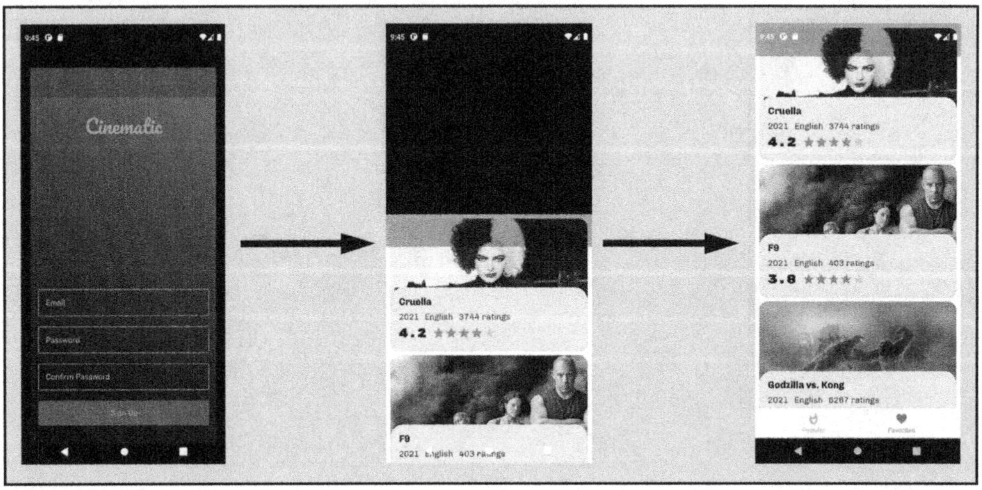

Easing the animation

Now, it's time to tackle the linear motion. You'll use an interpolator to add some easing to the animation to make it feel more natural. The `AccelerateDecelerate` interpolator is a particularly good fit here. It'll cause the motion to accelerate as the animation continues, then quickly decelerate before the end of the animation.

In **auth_main_enter.xml**, add the following line in the `set` declaration header, below the `startOffset` line:

```
android:interpolator="@android:anim/
accelerate_decelerate_interpolator"
```

The same interpolator will also improve the exit animation. Open **auth_main_exit.xml** and add the interpolator to the set declaration as well.

```
android:interpolator="@android:anim/
accelerate_decelerate_interpolator"
```

Run the app again. It's subtle, but the interpolator adds a nice bit of polish that makes the animation feel more natural.

Your next goal is to apply the same transitions when navigating from the main activity back to the authorization activity.

Transitioning on back press

At this point, you've nearly finished your fancy new activity animations. However, the animation only plays when you navigate from the authorization activity to the main activity. Ideally, the same animation sequence would run when the user taps the back button to go from the main activity to the authorization activity.

> **Note:** In a production app, you should set your login process up such that the user never "backs" into the login page, since they should stay logged in. This app has a fake login flow for the sake of emphasizing the animations.

To add an animation after a back press, you'll use `overridePendingTransition` again. This time, rather than calling it after a new activity starts, you'll call it after the main activity finishes.

Open **MainActivity.kt**. Add the following code below `onCreate`:

```
override fun finish() {
  super.finish()
  overridePendingTransition(R.anim.auth_main_enter,
R.anim.auth_main_exit)
}
```

Here, you override `finish` so you can apply the animations after the activity finishes.

Build and run the app. Navigate to the main activity, then press the back button to transition back to the authorization activity. You'll see the same animation.

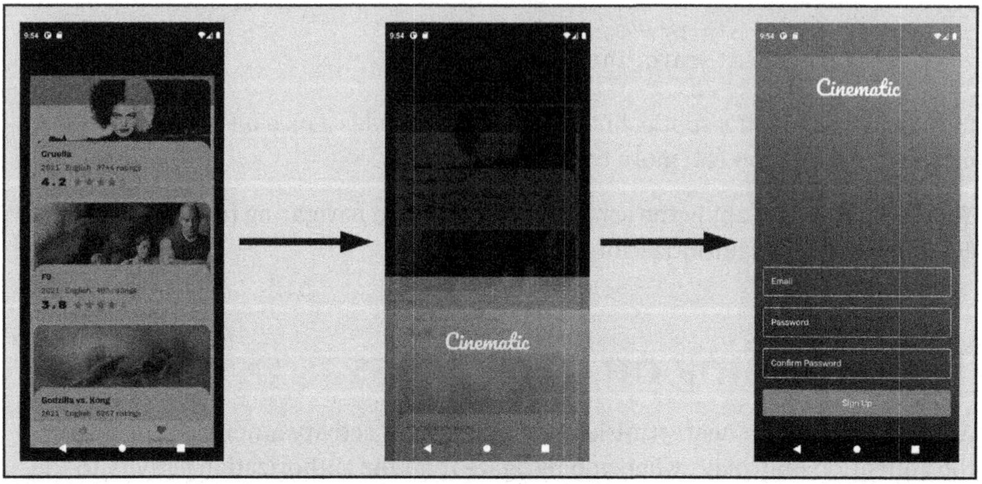

Now that you've made the transition from the authorization to the main screen beautiful, you'll add the same treatment to the transition from the main screen to the detail screen using the navigation component's animation support.

Using architecture component animations

Run the app and navigate to the main movie list screen. Now, tap one of the movies. You'll go to the movie details page, but there's no transition or animation; you'll change that now.

To do this, you'll build a fairly simple animation. Your goal is to have the details screen slide in from the right, while the movies list screen slides slightly to the left and fades away. It will look like the details screen slides in over the movie list screen.

Before you start writing the animations, you need to understand how the Android navigation component applies to animations.

The anatomy of a navigation component animation

The Android navigation component works by building up a graph of fragments with connections between each other. Those connections are called actions, and you use them to trigger navigation from one fragment to another.

Each action holds the key to animating the transition. Just like activity animations, actions can have enter and exit animations.

However, in addition to exit and enter animations, you can also specify **popEnter** and **popExit** animations. Here's a quick breakdown of the four different transition types:

- **exitAnim**: The **exit** animation governs the **exiting** fragment when you manually navigate from one fragment to another. So if you triggered a navigation action from `PopularMoviesFragment` to `MovieDetailsFragment`, `exitAnim` would govern how `PopularMoviesFragment` exits.

- **enterAnim**: The **enter** animation governs the **entering** fragment when you manually navigate from one fragment to another. In the example from the previous bullet, `enterAnim` would govern how `MovieDetailsFragment` enters.

- **popEnterAnim**: The **pop enter** animation is triggered when you pop the fragment back stack. It applies to the fragment that is re-entering the screen. So when you navigate from `PopularMoviesFragment` to `MovieDetailsFragment` and then tap back, the pop enter animation governs how `PopularMoviesFragment` comes *back* into the view.

- **popExitAnim**: The **pop exit** animation works similarly to the pop enter animation, except that it governs the animation for the fragment now **exiting** the view. So in the example above, the pop exit animation governs how `MovieDetailsFragment` leaves the view.

Now that you know all about how navigation component animations work, it's time to dive in and create the enter and exit animations for Cinematic.

Creating the enter and exit fragment animations

Open the **nav_graph_enter** animation file in the **anim** resource directory. Just like before, it's currently an empty `set`.

Remember, the enter animation governs the animation of the incoming fragment when you manually trigger a navigation event. That means that this animation governs `MovieDetailsFragment` when the user taps a movie in `PopularMoviesFragment`. When that happens, you want `MovieDetailsFragment` to slide in from the right.

The only animation you'll need is a simple call to `translate`. Replace the empty `set` with the following:

```
<translate xmlns:android="http://schemas.android.com/apk/res/
android"
  android:interpolator="@android:anim/
accelerate_decelerate_interpolator"
  android:fromXDelta="100%p"
  android:toXDelta="0"
  android:duration="@android:integer/config_mediumAnimTime" />
```

In the code above, you specify a `fromXDelta` value of **100%p**, which means this animation will start by translating the view 100% of the screen width to the right. So the view will be off-screen on the right when it starts.

You then specify a `toXDelta` value of **0**, meaning the view will slide back in from the left side of the screen, then stop.

Last but not least, you use `AccelerateDecelerateInterpolator` again to make the motion feel more natural.

Creating the exit animation for the fragment

Next, open the **nav_graph_exit** file in the **anim** resource directory. Again, it's an empty `set`.

For the exit animation, you want the fragment to slide slightly to the left while fading out. You'll use the `translate` and `alpha` animations to achieve that effect.

Start by adding the following block inside the body of the `set`:

```
<translate
  android:fromXDelta="0"
  android:toXDelta="-20%p"
  android:duration="@android:integer/config_longAnimTime"/>
```

Since this animation will govern `PopularMoviesFragment` when it leaves the view, you set `fromXDelta` to **0**, meaning the animation won't move the view initially. You then translate the view 20% to the left by using **-20%p** for `toXDelta`.

Next, add the alpha animation below the `translate` block:

```
<alpha
  android:fromAlpha="1.0"
  android:toAlpha="0.0"
  android:duration="@android:integer/config_mediumAnimTime" />
```

The alpha animation is pretty straightforward. While the animation is running, you fade from full alpha tozero alpha.

Now that you've set up the enter and exit animations, it's time to wire them up and see how it looks.

Setting the navigation component animations

Open **nav_graph.xml** in **res/navigation**. Tap the connection between the **popularMoviesFragment** and **movieDetailsFragment** views.

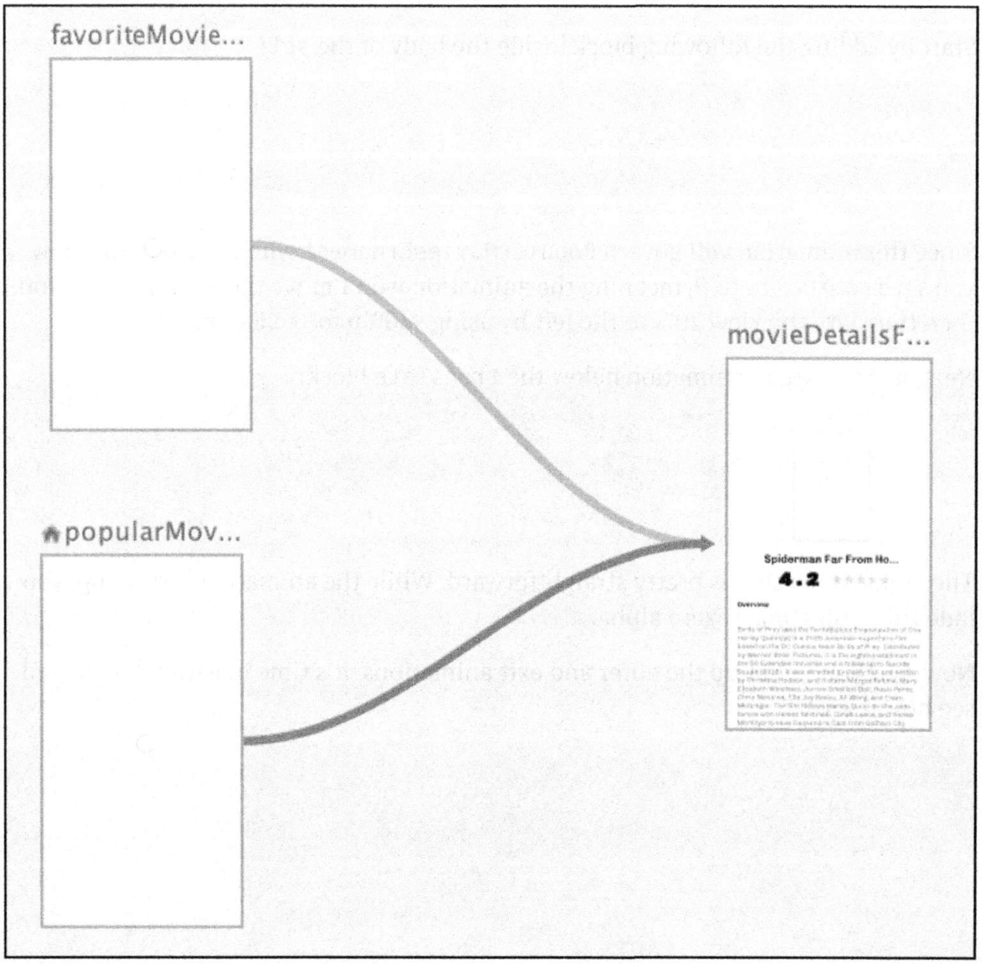

Now that you've selected the connection, add **nav_graph_exit** and **nav_graph_enter** in the **exitAnim** and **enterAnim** sections of the attribute window.

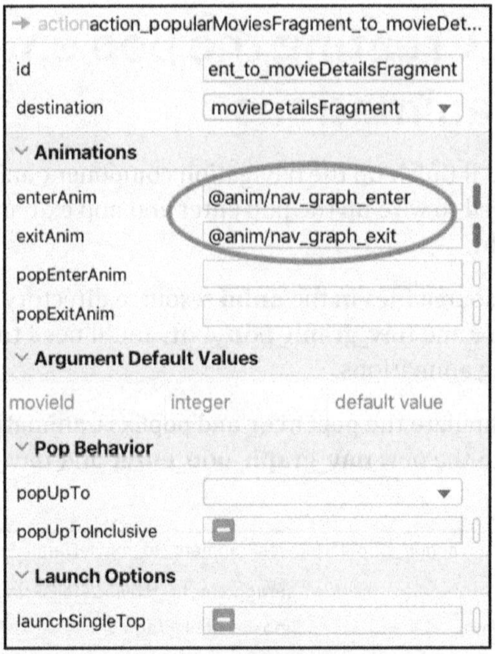

Now, build and run the app. Navigate to the popular movies list and tap a movie. You'll see the details screen slide in from the right while the popular movies screen slides to the left and fades away.

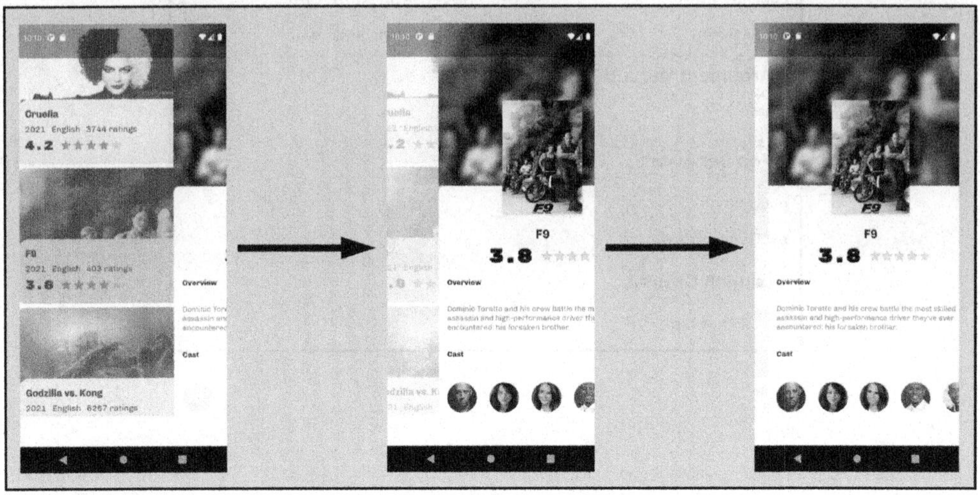

However, if you go back from the movie details page, no animation runs and the details page just disappears. You'll fix that in the challenge section!

Challenge: Creating the pop enter and pop exit detail animations

In this challenge, you'll finish up the navigation component animations you started earlier. You'll first need to wire up the pop enter and pop exit animations in the navigation component.

There's two ANIM resource files in the **anim** resource directory named **nav_graph_pop_enter** and **nav_graph_pop_exit**. You'll need to use these two files to handle the popping animations.

In **nav_graph.xml** populate the `popEnter` and `popExit` animation fields in the attribute window with the new **nav_graph_pop_enter** and **nav_graph_pop_exit** resource files.

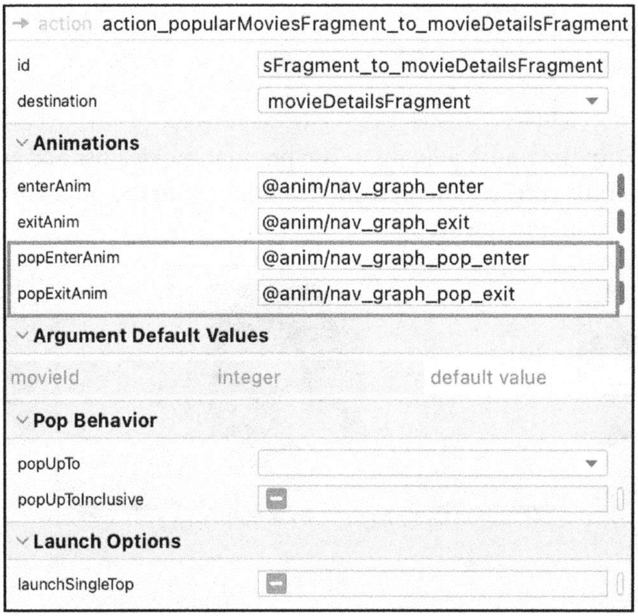

You'll first need to add an animation to the **nav_graph_pop_exit.xml** file. Remember that the pop exit animation runs when the user pops a fragment off the back stack, so this animation will run when the user is on the details fragment screen and taps the back button. The animation should translate the details screen off of the screen to the right, so you'll need to use the translate tag.

After adding the pop exit animation, you'll then need to add the pop enter animation to the **nav_graph_pop_exit.xml** file. It again makes sense to reverse the movie list entrance animation, so you'll want to both translate the movies list screen to the right while also fading it back in. You'll have to use both the translate and alpha tags in a set to achieve the desired animation!

Once your animation is all finished, it should look like this:

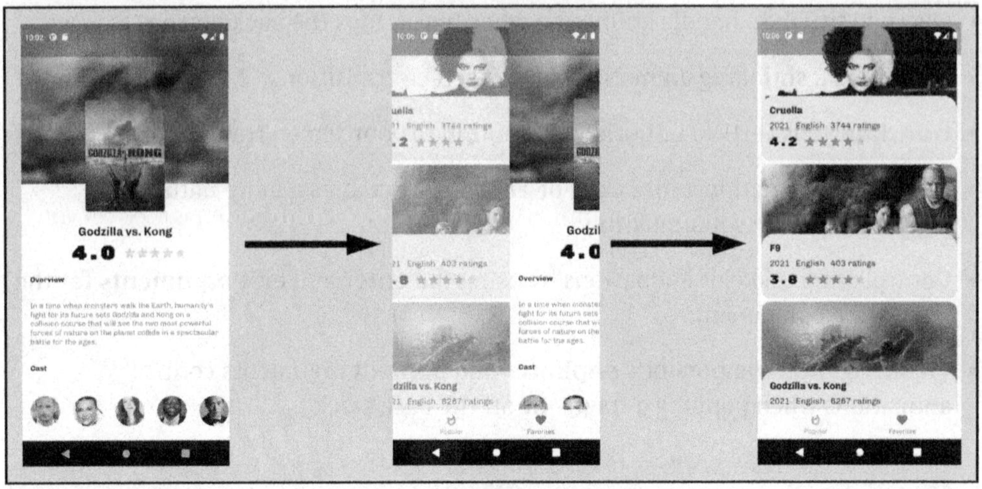

Well done on completing this chapter! Learning to animate fragment and activity transitions is a complex topic. You've gotten a taste in this chapter, but you'll learn more about the subject in the following chapters as well.

Key points

- Use **overridePendingTransition** for activity animations.
- If you're outside the activity, use **ActivityOptions.makeCustomAnimation**.
- Combine sets of animations using the `set` tag.
- Use **startOffset** to emphasize one animation over another.
- To make screen transitions feel more natural, use **interpolators**.
- Use enter and exit animations to give your app a more complex and cohesive feeling.
- Override **finish** to handle animating when a user taps the back button.
- **scale** adds a shrinking animation to your screen transitions.
- **translate** adds vertical or horizontal motion to your screen transitions.
- **alpha**, in conjunction with `scale` or `translate`, creates a more natural and pleasing enter or exit animation.
- Control enter and exit animations by using the **enter** and **exit arguments** for the navigation component.
- The navigation component's **popEnter** and **popExit** arguments control animations when popping a fragment off the back stack.

Where to go from here?

You've learned a lot about how to create beautiful animations when transitioning between activities or fragments. You animated the transition when the app uses Navigation Controller. To learn more about the Navigation Controller, check out the course https://www.raywenderlich.com/21959768-jetpack-navigation-getting-started. There are many different ways to combine the tools you've learned to make creative and fancy animations, so feel free to play around with them to create something beautiful.

In the next chapter, you'll see how to use the transition framework to create beautiful fragment-to-fragment transitions. See you there!

Chapter 5: Transition Framework

By Alex Sullivan

In the previous chapter, you learned all about using `anim` resource files to animate between different activities and fragments. But while you can create beautiful screen-to-screen animations that way, sometimes you want to apply different animations to specific views and create more complex behavior when transitioning between fragments or activities. That's where the **Transition** framework comes into play.

In this chapter, you'll:

- Learn what the **Transition** framework is and how it differs from `anim` resource files.
- Programmatically create transition animation objects to animate between fragments.
- Create complex transitions using transition sets.
- Troubleshoot common pitfalls when using the **Transition** framework.

Introducing the Transition framework

The **Transition** framework is *yet another* animation framework you can use when building Android apps. Unlike the other animation frameworks you've learned about, you use the transition framework on entire `ViewGroups` to animate either changes in visibility throughout the `ViewGroups` children or to animate complete changes to the `ViewGroup`'s structure. So rather than focusing on one specific `View` to animate, you use Transition to build animations for changes to a whole set of `Views`. This makes it easy to do things like animate changes to a view's visibility or create complex and beautiful fragment and activity animations!

Just as with the **Animation** and **Animator** frameworks, you can use the transition framework by either creating static XML files or programmatically instantiating `Transition` objects. In this chapter, you'll focus on using transitions programmatically to define `Fragment` animations when switching between the `AuthFragment`, `SignupFragment` and `LoginFragment` objects.

The anatomy of a Fragment transition

In Chapter 4, "Animating Activity & Fragment Transitions With XML", you learned how to apply navigation component fragment animations by using the `enterAnim`, `exitAnim`, `popEnterAnim` and `popExitAnim` fields in **nav_graph.xml**. The flow is similar when you use the transition framework, except you apply the animation arguments on the actual `Fragment` instead of in the navigation graph XML file.

> **Note**: Unfortunately, you can't use the **Transition** framework for fragment animations if you're using the Jetpack Navigation library — only if you're manually managing the fragment back stack yourself. Working with Jetpack limits you to the `anim` resource files you learned about in Chapter 3, "XML Animations", and Chapter 4, "Animating Activity & Fragment Transitions With XML".

`Fragment` exposes four relevant methods for applying `Transitions`:

- **exitTransition**: Governs the animation that runs when the user navigates *away* from this `Fragment`.
- **enterTransition**: Governs the animation that runs when this `Fragment` displays for the first time.
- **reenterTransition**: Governs the animation that runs when this `Fragment` reappears after another fragment pops off the back stack. It's similar to `popEnterAnim` from the Jetpack navigation library.
- **returnTransition**: Governs the animation that runs when hiding this `Fragment` after it's popped off the back stack. It's similar to `popExitAnim` from the Jetpack navigation library.

You'll get the chance to use each of these methods later in this chapter. Now that you know how to set transitions on a `Fragment`, it's time to add your first transition!

Creating a fade transition

The first animation you'll build with the transition framework is a simple fade between the `AuthFragment` and the `SignupFragment`. The user triggers this animation by tapping the **I'm new to Cinematic** button on the initial authorization screen.

To create this animation, you need to set the `exitTransition` in `AuthFragment` and the `enterTransition` in `SignupFragment`.

Start by opening **AuthFragment.kt** and overriding `onCreate`:

```
override fun onCreate(savedInstanceState: Bundle?) {
  super.onCreate(savedInstanceState)
}
```

You'll encapsulate the transition logic in one place by adding all your transition code to `onCreate`.

Now that you have a method to contain your transition logic, it's time to create the fade animation. Add the following below the call to `super.onCreate` in the `onCreate` you just added:

```
exitTransition = Fade()
```

> **Note**: Make sure to import the `androidX` version of the `Fade` transition. The Transition framework, like many other classes in Android, has two versions: platform and AndroidX. The AndroidX version is regularly updated and much less buggy.

Here, you set the `exitTransition` property of the `Fragment` to the `Fade` transition. `Fade` is a simple transition that fades the alpha of the layout in or out depending on how the layout changes. When the layout goes from hidden to shown, `Fade` fades the layout in. Alternatively, if the visibility changes from shown to hidden, `Fade` fades the layout out.

Next, you need to add some similar code to `SignupFragment`.

Fading the signup screen in

Now that you've set the `exitTransition` on `AuthFragment`, it's time to do the same song and dance in `SignupFragment`. Start by opening **SignupFragment.kt** and overriding `onCreate`:

```
override fun onCreate(savedInstanceState: Bundle?) {
  super.onCreate(savedInstanceState)
}
```

Next, set `enterTransition`:

```
enterTransition = Fade()
```

Since you want `SignupFragment` to fade *in*, you set the `enterTransition` field.

Build and run, then tap the **I'm new to Cinematic** button. You'll see the following animation:

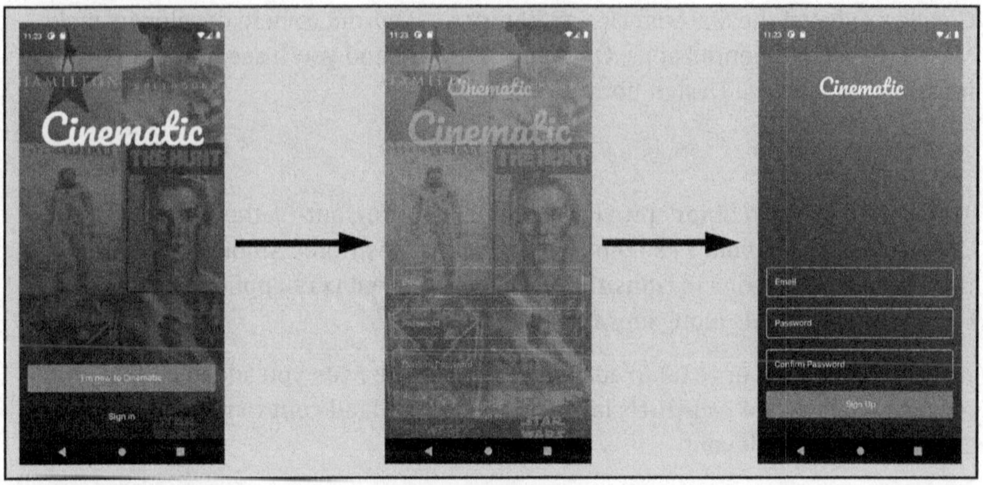

Now, tap the **back** button. You'll see the same animation, but in reverse: `SignupFragment` fades out while `AuthFragment` fades in.

That's great! But why is it happening? You didn't set the `reenterTransition` or `returnTransition` arguments, so why do you have an animation when you pop `SignupFragment` off the back stack?

A `Fragment` will default to using the same transition for the `reenterTransition` as for the `exitTransition`. It also defaults to using the same transition for the `returnTransition` as for the `enterTransition`. Since the `Fade` transition fades views in or out depending on the visibility change, the return animation looks the way you'd expect. Woohoo, free animations!

The fade animation looks fine, but it'd be great to add something just a bit snazzier so the app feels professional. Luckily, you can leverage transitions from the Material Design library for some beautiful and subtle animations!

Using Material Design transitions

Google produced the Material Design library for Android to help developers make Material Design-oriented apps. Open **build.gradle** and you'll see that it already includes the Material Design library:

```
implementation 'com.google.android.material:material:1.3.0'
```

The Material Design library provides several beautiful, out-of-the-box transitions that you can use in your `Fragment` or `Activity` transitions. Among the snazziest is the `MaterialSharedAxis` transition. `MaterialSharedAxis` applies a subtle slide combined with a fade along any axis you want.

Next, you'll use `MaterialSharedAxis` to replace the `Fade` you added earlier. Your goal is to have `AuthFragment`'s layout slide over and fade out to reveal `SignupFragment`'s layout.

Start by opening **AuthFragment.kt** and replacing the `Fade` transition with a `MaterialSharedAxis` transition:

```
exitTransition = MaterialSharedAxis(MaterialSharedAxis.X, true)
```

> **Note**: When importing the library, select `com.google.android.material.transition.MaterialSharedAxis`.

`MaterialSharedAxis` takes two arguments:

1. The axis along which the animation should slide. In this case, you want to slide the view out on the horizontal axis, so you've provided the X-axis here.
2. A Boolean value indicating whether the transition should slide left or right along the X-axis. `True` indicates the view should slide left, while `false` indicates it should slide right. Here, you provide `true` because you want the layout to slide out to the left.

Next, open **SignupFragment.kt** and delete the line declaring the `enterTransition`. Since the goal is to have the `AuthFragment` view slide and fade out to reveal the `SignupFragment` view, you don't need a transition for the `SignupFragment` — it will just appear as `AuthFragment` slides out.

Now, build and run the app and tap the **I'm new to Cinematic** button. You'll see the following animation:

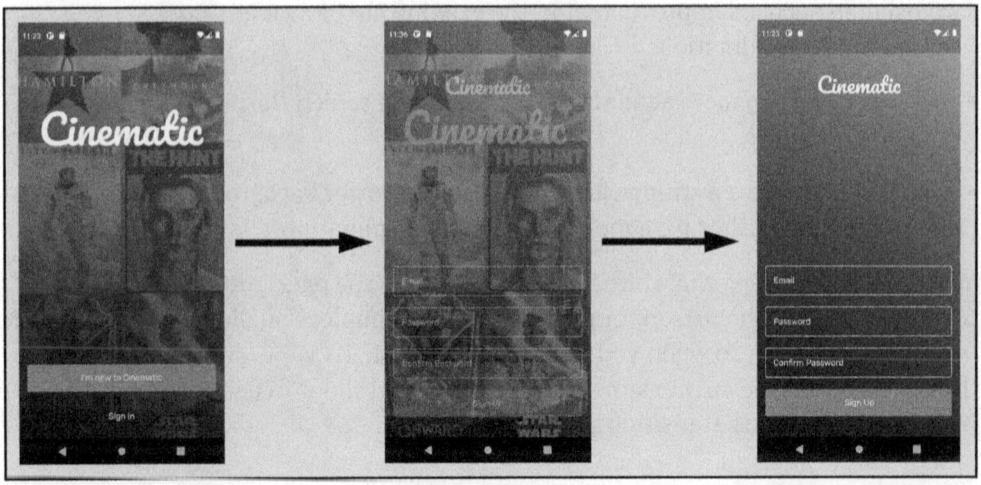

The animation looks good, but it's a bit quick. Ideally, `AuthFragment` should take just a touch longer to animate out so the user sees the full effect of the animation. You can fix this by using `setDuration`, which is exposed on `Transition`, to update the animation's duration.

Back in `AuthFragment`, add the `apply` block to the end of the line:

```
exitTransition = MaterialSharedAxis(MaterialSharedAxis.X,
true).apply {
  duration = 1000
}
```

This sets the duration on the `MaterialSharedAxis` exit transition.

Now, build and run again. The animation is slower and feels more deliberate.

The animation looks solid so far, but you still need to do some cleanup work.

Cleaning up the material transition

Two major areas need improvement in the existing `AuthFragment`-to-`SignupFragment` animation:

- When you tap `SignupFragment`'s back button, the screen flashes white instead of animating cleanly.
- Sometimes, you see a strange artifact where the poster background in the `AuthFragment` flashes for a moment during the animation.

You'll start by tackling the white flash when you tap the back button on `SignupFragment`. The reason for the flash is quite simple: You didn't set a transition in `SignupFragment`, so when you tap the back button, its view immediately disappears. Then the `AuthFragment`'s view fades and slides in using the `MaterialSharedAxis` transition you defined earlier.

> **Note**: Remember that a `Fragment` will use the `exitTransition` that you set as the `reenterTransition` if you didn't set a `reenterTransition` manually. That's why you're using the `MaterialSharedAxis` transition you defined as the `exitTransition` for the `reenterTransition`!

To fix the white flash, you'll need to define a `returnTransition` on the `SignupFragment`.

Add the following in `SignupFragment`'s `onCreate`:

```
returnTransition = MaterialSharedAxis(MaterialSharedAxis.X,
false).apply {
  duration = 1000
}
```

You're again using a `MaterialSharedAxis` on the X-axis with a duration of 1,000 milliseconds. This time, you're setting the `forward` field to `false` so the `SignupFragment` view animates to the *right* instead of the left when the user pops `SignupFragment`.

Build and run again. You'll see an animation that looks like this:

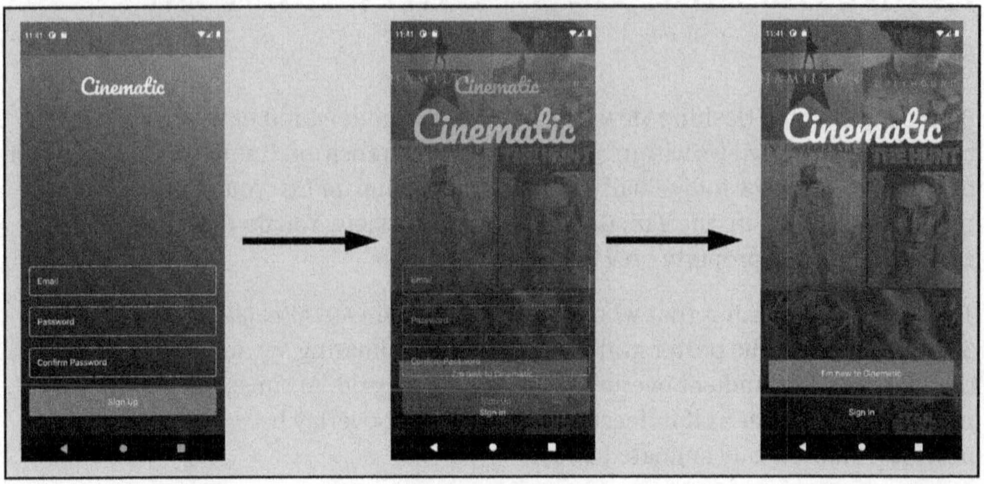

Look at that! That is one terrible-looking animation. What gives?

It's hard to pinpoint, but what's happening here is that the `SignupFragments` view is sliding out to the right while the `AuthFragments` view is sliding in from the right. The result is a jarring animation that leaves a lot of empty space while the two animations are running. That's not what you want — you want the `AuthFragments` view to slide in **from the left** rather than from the right.

`AuthFragments` view slides in from the right because it's using the same transition for the `reenter` transition as you specified for the `exitTransition`. Unfortunately, `MaterialSharedAxis` doesn't care whether the view is animating in or out when it comes to the direction of the slide — it's entirely driven by the `forward` argument.

You'll solve this problem by providing a `reenterTransition` in `AuthFragment` manually, then setting the `forward` argument to `false`. Add the following below the line setting the `exitTransition` in `AuthFragment`:

```
reenterTransition = MaterialSharedAxis(MaterialSharedAxis.X,
false)
```

The above code adds the `reenterTransition` to the `AuthFragment`. Now, build and run again. You'll see a much more pleasing and consistent animation. Next, you need to tackle how `AuthFragments` poster image flashes during the animation!

Fixing flashing views with transition groups

Before tackling the flashing view bug, you need to understand how a transition typically animates views within a `ViewGroup`. The transition framework will attempt to animate each view individually within a `ViewGroup` *unless* you tell the system that it should animate the `ViewGroup` as a singular view. You do that using the `transitionGroup` property on `ViewGroup`.

The cause of the flash is that when you navigate from `AuthFragment` to `SignupFragment`, the poster grid's `ImageView` is animating separately from the `View` that provides the gradient overlay above the poster grid. At times, that causes the poster grid to appear as if it doesn't have a gradient overlay because the view that provides it has already animated away.

To fix this issue, you need to set `android:transitionGroup` on the `ViewGroup` that contains the poster grid and the overlay.

Start by opening **fragment_auth.xml** and navigating to the `FrameLayout` that contains the poster grid `ImageView` and the gradient `View`.

Next, add the following line below the `layout_height` declaration in the `FrameLayout` tag:

```
android:transitionGroup="true"
```

Now, the `FrameLayout` acts as a single unit while it transitions. You won't see the temporary flash of the poster grid without the gradient overlay anymore, since the two will always be in sync.

Run the app again and tap the **I'm new to Cinematic** button. You'll see a pristine animation.

At this point, your animation looks great, but you know what would be even better? If you did something funky with Cinematic's title!

Animating individual views

One of the coolest things about the transition framework is that you can target individual views to run different animations. For this app, you'll add a special animation to the Cinematic `TextView` so it slides up in the `AuthFragment` exit transition and slides back down in the `SignupFragment` enter transition.

You want to add this slide while also preserving the existing `MaterialSharedAxis` transition. To do this, you need to use a new tool in thetransition framework toolkit: **transition sets**.

Combining transitions with transition sets

A `TransitionSet` is a special transition that acts as a container for multiple other transitions. You can think of it as the transition framework version of the `AnimationSet` utility you used in Chapter 4, "Animating Activity & Fragment Transitions With XML". Here, you'll use a `TransitionSet` to combine the `MaterialSharedAxis` transition with a new `Slide` transition to achieve the animation you want.

Start by opening **AuthFragment.kt** and creating a new `TransitionSet` below the call to `super.onCreate()`:

```
val exitTransitionSet = TransitionSet().apply {

}
```

Don't worry about the empty `apply` block; you'll use it later to populate the `exitTransitionSet`.

Next, create a new variable for the `MaterialSharedAxis` transition that you're currently using for the `exitTransition`, above the `exitTransitionSet` declaration:

```
val materialSlideOut = MaterialSharedAxis(MaterialSharedAxis.X,
true).apply {
  duration = 1000
}
```

You'll add the materialSlideOut transition to your exitTransitionSet in just a moment. But before you do, create one last transition above the materialSlideOut declaration — the Slide transition that will slide your title TextView up:

```
val logoSlideUp = Slide(Gravity.TOP).apply {
  duration = 700
}
```

Slide is a Transition that works exactly as you'd expect it to: It slides the view in whichever direction you specify in the constructor. In this case, you want the logo to slide up, so you pass in Gravity.TOP.

Now that you've specified your transitions, you can add them all to the exitTransitionSet by placing the following commands into the apply block:

```
addTransition(materialSlideOut)
addTransition(logoSlideUp)
```

TransitionSets can play the transitions either together or one after the other. In this app, you want the MaterialSharedAxis and Slide transitions to happen at the same time, so add the following in the apply block of exitTransitionSet:

```
ordering = TransitionSet.ORDERING_TOGETHER
```

> **Note**: If you wanted the transitions to play sequentially, you'd use TransitionSet.ORDERING_SEQUENTIAL instead.

Now that your exitTransitionSet is ready to go, replace the old exitTransition with the following code:

```
exitTransition = exitTransitionSet
```

This assigns your exitTransitionSet as the transition to run when the Fragment exits.

You're 99% of the way towards achieving some next-level transitions. But you still have to make sure that the Slide transition only targets the logo's TextView. To do that, you'll use the excludeTarget and addTarget APIs.

Targeting a specific view in a transition

Now that you've defined your transitions, all that's left is to make sure the `Slide` transition only runs for the logo `TextView` while the `MaterialSharedAxis` transition runs for everything else.

To achieve that goal, you'll use two new methods on a `Transition`:

- **excludeTarget**: Tells the transition **not** to run on the given `View`.
- **addTarget**: Tells the transition to **only** run on the provided `View(s)`.

First, you want to make sure that the `MaterialSharedAxis` transition *doesn't* run on the logo `TextView`. You want the logo `TextView` to slide up, not slide to the side and fade out.

Add the following call in the `apply` block of the `materialSlideOut` declaration:

```
excludeTarget(R.id.logo, true)
```

The `excludeTarget` call will ensure that the `MaterialSharedAxis` transition will **not** run on the logo `TextView`. Pretty easy, huh?

Next, you need to make sure that the `Slide` transition *only* runs on the logo `TextView`. Add the following in the `apply` block of the `logoSlideUp` transition:

```
addTarget(R.id.logo)
```

As mentioned earlier, the `addTarget` call will force the given `Transition` to *only* run on the targets that you've added. You can add as many targets as you want; you don't have to stick to just one `View`. Calling `addTarget` modifies the behavior of the `Transition` pretty heavily — normally, a `Transition` will operate on *all* the `Views` in the `Fragment`. As soon as you call `addTarget`, you change the behavior so it now *only* operates on the `Views` you've added.

Build and run the app. You'll see the Cinematic logo slide up while the rest of the layout slides to the left and fades out like normal. Nice!

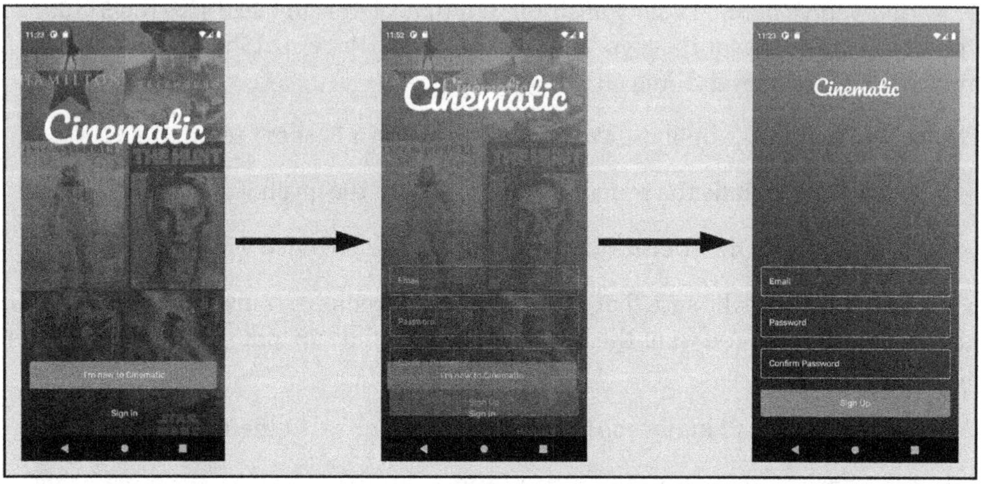

Sliding the logo view back down

The only thing left to do to finish this beautiful animation is to have the logo `TextView` slide *down* when you get to the `SignupFragment`.

To do that, you'll need to add a `Slide` enter transition, then use the `addTarget` API to target the logo `TextView`.

Open `SignupFragment`, then add the following below the call to `super.onCreate()`:

```
enterTransition =
Slide(Gravity.TOP).addTarget(R.id.signup_logo).setDuration(700)
```

Since the only enter transition will be the logo sliding *down*, you don't need to use a `TransitionSet`. Instead, just create a new `Slide` transition that will slide down from the `TOP`, targeting the `signup_logo` `TextView`, then set the duration to 700 milliseconds.

Now, build and run and tap the sign-up button. The logo slides up on the `AuthFragment` screen, but the logo doesn't slide down in the `SignupFragment` screen. What gives?

Well, you know those times when you're building an Android app and you say to yourself, "Wow, this API is working exactly as I expected it to!"? This isn't one of those times.

Recall that you can use the `transitionGroup` flag to specify that a `ViewGroup` should transition as one singular unit. There are some hidden... complexities there that you haven't touched on yet. Specifically, that flag will be **automatically set to true** if you set a background for the `ViewGroup`.

Open **fragment_signup.xml**. If you look at the top-level `ConstraintLayout` in the file, you'll see that it does, indeed, have a background. That means the transition framework is treating that `ConstraintLayout` as one single unit — and animating it as a single unit as well.

It also means that the transition framework will **ignore** any transitions that target a `View` within the `ViewGroup`, since that `ViewGroup` is animating as one cohesive item. Animating a subview would break that behavior.

To fix the issue and see the logo slide, you need to specify that the top-level `ConstraintLayout` should **not** operate as a single group. Add the following to the `ConstraintLayouts` declaration:

```
android:transitionGroup="false"
```

Now build and run. The logo will slide in and out as you expected:

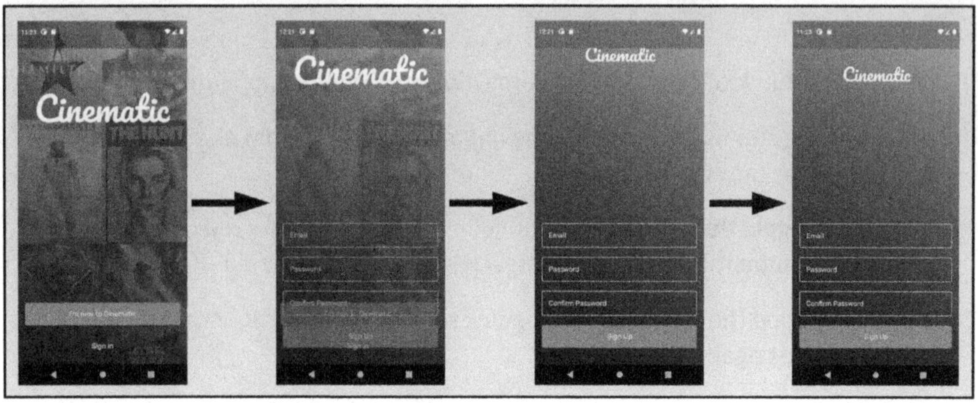

There's only one problem — the white flash is back when you back out of the `SignupFragment`! You'll fix that next by modifying the logic that decides when the view should act as a transition group.

Changing the transition group logic

The screen flashes because, now that the layout isn't a transition group, the top-level layout fades out at a different time than the other views on the screen. Because the top-level layout contains the background for the screen, you see the bare white screen exposed behind it.

To fix the issue, you need to toggle the transition group logic when the user taps the back button. You'll do this by setting the `transitionGroup` flag programmatically when the user goes back.

In **SignupFragment.kt**, add the following below the block of code setting the click listener on the sign-up button in `onCreateView`:

```
// 1
activity?.onBackPressedDispatcher?.addCallback(viewLifecycleOwne
r) {
  // 2
  binding.root.isTransitionGroup = true
  // 3
  parentFragmentManager.popBackStack()
}
```

That's a dense chunk of code. Here's a breakdown of what's happening:

1. First, you register a callback with the `onBackPressedDispatcher` to notify you when the user taps the back button.
2. Then, you toggle the `isTransitionGroup` flag on the root `View` of the layout to `true` so the animation will run as expected.
3. Finally, you pop the `Fragment` back stack to pop `SignupFragment` and show `AuthFragment` again.

Run the app again. Tap the sign-up button, then use the back button. The result will be a beautiful forward *and* backward animation.

Congratulations! You've finished designing an elegant, subtle and meaningful animation using the Transition framework.

Challenges

Challenge 1: Add transition animations to LoginFragment

Right now, the animations run beautifully when you navigate from `AuthFragment` to `SignupFragment`, but the `LoginFragment` doesn't have any transitions. As a result, the animation looks off when you navigate from `AuthFragment` to `LoginFragment`. In this challenge, you'll update the `LoginFragment` to show the same animations as you used for `SignupFragment`.

First, you need to override `onCreate` in `LoginFragment`, just as you did for `AuthFragment` and `SignupFragment`.

Then, you'll set the `enterTransition` to a `Slide` that targets the logo.

Next, you'll override the `returnTransition` to be a `MaterialSharedAxis` transition, as in `SignupFragment`.

You'll also need to set the `transitionGroup` parameter to `false` in **fragment_login.xml** to make the `Slide` work.

Finally, to avoid the white flash when you back out of the `LoginFragment`, you'll need to add a back-press listener once again, then disable the `transitionGroup` in the root layout when the user taps the back button.

Challenge 2: Add a fade transition to work with the logo slide transition

Now that the logo slides in on both the `LoginFragment` and `SignupFragment`, you can take it one step farther! In this challenge, you'll have the logo slide in while *also* fading in.

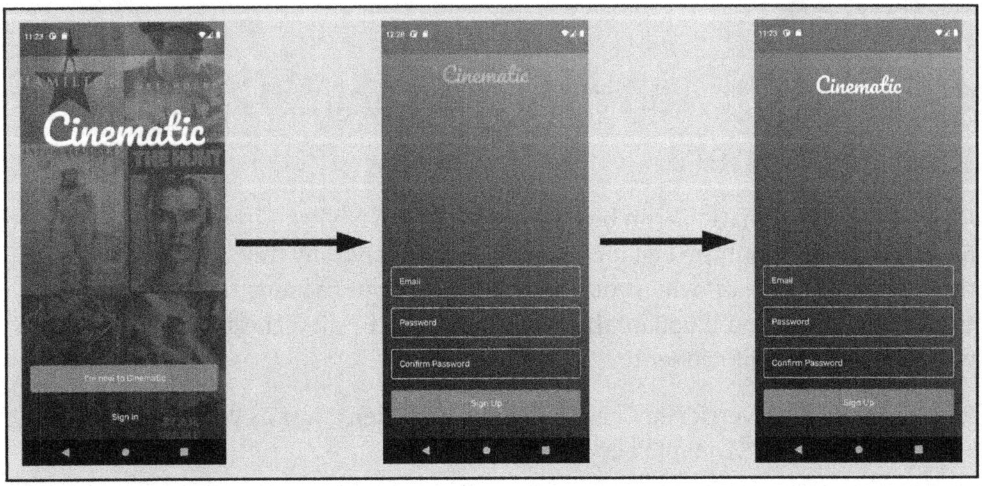

First, you need to define a `TransitionSet` to contain both the `Slide` transition and a new `Fade` transition.

Then, you'll pull out the `Slide` transition into its own variable. After that, you'll need to add another variable representing a `Fade` transition. Both should target the logo `TextView` — either `signup_logo` or `login_logo`, depending on the class.

You'll then add both those transitions to the `TransitionSet` and set the `TransitionSet` as the enter transition.

To make the fade animation a bit more noticeable, set the duration of the `Fade` to be slightly longer than the duration of the `Slide`. 1,000 milliseconds for the `Slide` and 2,000 milliseconds for the `Fade` works well!

You can find the solution to the challenges above in the **challenges** folder.

Key points

- The Transition framework is an alternative way to create beautiful `Fragment` and `Activity` animations.
- Make sure to use the AndroidX version of the transition framework, rather than the platform version.
- You can use the `enterTransition/exitTransition/reenterTransition/returnTransition` properties on `Fragment` to set transitions for different `Fragment` scenarios.
- Use the Material Design library and the `MaterialSharedAxis` transition for some easy animation wins.
- `TransitionSet` lets you combine multiple transitions.
- You can also use `Fade` and `Slide` to easily fade and slide views into the scene.
- Target individual views with the `addTarget` API.
- Remove individual views from a given transition by using the `remoteTarget` API.
- If you want a `ViewGroup` to animate as one unit, set the `transitionGroup` flag in XML or the `isTransitionGroup` property in code.
- If you see strange behavior like white flashes or views not animating, there's a good chance you need to tweak the `transitionGroup` property.

Now get ready! In the next chapter you'll be adding some motion to **Cinematic** using **Element Transitions**!

Chapter 6: Element Transitions

By Alex Sullivan

You've learned about a lot of different types of screen transitions so far, but the coolest is still to come! Motion is the name of the game when building animations, and one of the coolest pieces of motion you can introduce in your apps is the **shared element transition**. A common place for shared element transition is transitioning from a list item to detail view. The user's eye can be drawn to certain shared elements in the fragments, instead of transitioning the entire view heirarchy with an enter or exit transition.

In this chapter, you'll learn:

- What a shared element transition is.
- How to use a shared element transition when changing fragments.
- How to use custom transitions to make your shared element transition beautiful.
- What a circular reveal animation is and how to use it to reveal tab content.

Now, it's time to jump right in!

Getting started

Using Android Studio Arctic Fox or newer, open the starter project within **06-element-transitions** in the **aat-materials** repository. Once the project syncs, build and run. You'll see the login screen.

By the end of this chapter, you'll have an app full of beautiful, meaningful screen animations!

Introduction to shared element transitions

Shared element transitions are a handy way to share a `View` between two different `Fragments` or `Activitys`. They make it seem as if a `View` is moving from one screen to another. These shared elements add a sense of continuity between screens.

They also help a user figure out where content went or how a new screen relates to the previous screen.

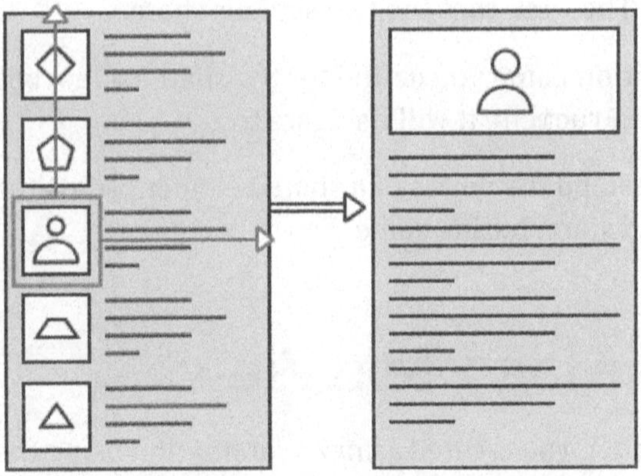

Even though shared element transitions make it *seem* like two screens are sharing a `View`, it's important to note that each screen still has its independent copy of the "shared" `View`. The shared element animation is just UI trickery; under the hood, you're still creating two normal layouts, each of which defines its `Views` internally.

Now that you understand what a shared element transition *is*, it's time to learn about their components.

Anatomy of a shared element transition

Shared element transitions consist of two key components:

1. The `View` to be "shared". If you're navigating from `Fragment` A to B, this will be a `View` in `Fragment` A.
2. The **transition name** of the shared `View`. The transition name is how you tie together the shared `Views`. The `View` in `Fragment` A needs to have the same transition name as the `View` in `Fragment` B for the shared element transition to work.

When building shared element transitions with `Fragments`, you use `addSharedElement`, a method on `FragmentTransaction`, to tell the framework to create the shared element transition. You typically call `addSharedElement` when building up your `FragmentTransaction` to swap out the currently displayed `Fragment`.

`addSharedElement` takes two parameters that map to the two key components outlined above:

- **sharedElement**: The `View` that the two screens share.
- **name**: The transition name you define for the shared `View`, both in the current `Fragment` and the `Fragment` it will navigate to.

Now that you understand the basics of a shared element transition, it's time to get your hands dirty and start sharing some views!

Sharing the logo TextView

In the previous chapter, you created a snazzy animation using the `Transition` framework that showed the Cinematic logo sliding up on the `AuthFragment` and then back down on the `SignupFragment` and `LoginFragment`.

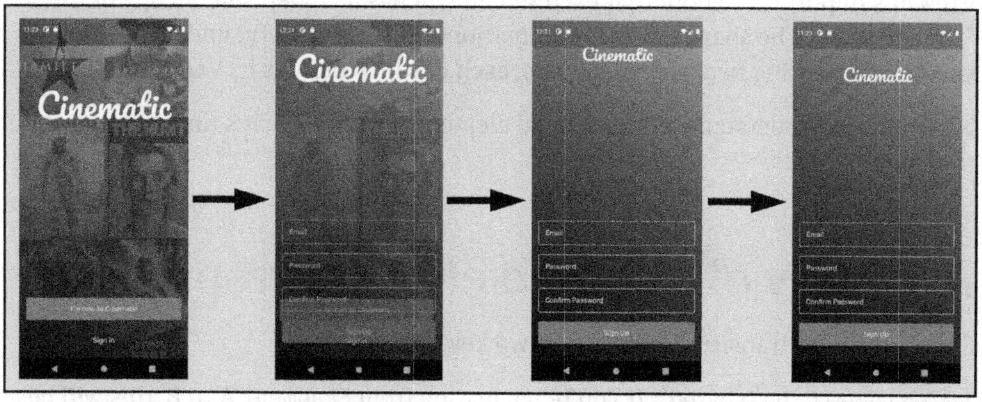

That transition looks pretty good — but it would look even better if the logo used a shared element transition.

You'll build a shared element transition to share the Cinematic logo `TextView` between `AuthFragment` and `SignupFragment`/`LoginFragment`. Here's how the desired animation should look:

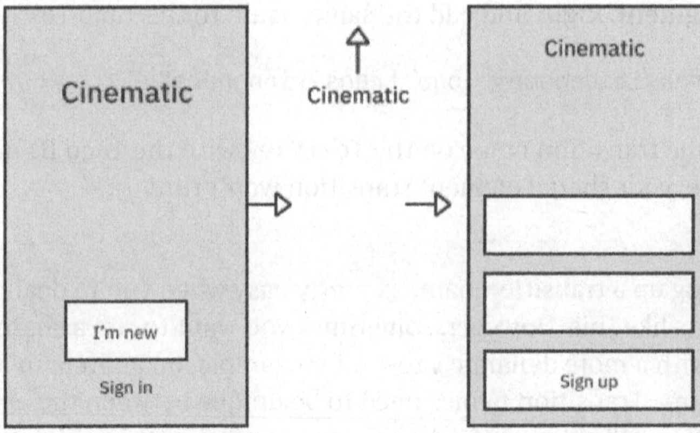

The next step in your shared element journey is to add a transition name to the logo `TextView`.

Defining a transition name

As a recap, the transition name is a property on a `View` that the system uses to match up your shared `Views`. It tells the framework that the two `Views` are linked and should run a shared element transition between them.

You'll define a transition name on the three logo `TextViews` across the `AuthFragment`, `LoginFragment` and `SignupFragment` screens.

Start by opening **fragment_auth.xml**. Find the `logo` `TextView` and add the following tag to its body:

```
android:transitionName="logo_transition_name"
```

Here, you set a transition name of **logo_transition_name** on the `TextView`.

Now, you need to do the same for both the **fragment_signup** and **fragment_login** files, to give them all the same transition name.

Open **fragment_signup** and add the transition name to `logo` `TextView`:

```
android:transitionName="logo_transition_name"
```

Next, open **fragment_login** and add the same, again to the `logo` `TextView`:

```
android:transitionName="logo_transition_name"
```

Be sure to set the transition name on the `TextView` with the `logo` ID in each of the files. Otherwise, your shared element transition won't run!

> **Note**: Setting up a transition name is pretty easy when you're dealing with static layouts like this. However, sometimes you want to run a shared element transition with a more dynamic `View` — for example, on an item in a `RecyclerView`. Transition names need to be unique between the elements of the shared `Views`. That means, when you're using something like a `RecyclerView`, you can't just set the transition name in XML because each item in the `RecyclerView` would have the same transition name; the framework wouldn't know which `Views` are being shared. In that scenario, you can programmatically set the `transitionName` to give each item in the `RecyclerView` has a unique transition name.

Now that you've defined your transition name, it's time to put the shared element transition to work!

Triggering the shared element transition

In Cinematic, `AuthActivity` manages the `Fragments` in the authorization flow. All the `Fragments` in the authorization flow share the `AuthViewModel` with `AuthActivity`. When the user taps a button that should cause `AuthActivity` to change the current `Fragment`, the `Fragment` that's currently displaying will call a method on `AuthViewModel`. Calling that method will trigger one of the `LiveData` objects to either change the `Fragment` or navigate to the main screen.

Open **AuthActivity.kt** and look at the bottom of onCreate. AuthActivity observes two LiveData objects to figure out when to transition between different fragments:

```
viewModel.showLogin.observe(this) {
  showLogin()
}
viewModel.showSignUp.observe(this) {
  showSignup()
}
```

showLogin and showSignup do the actual Fragment manipulation. That's where you'll need to add the call to addSharedElement to trigger the shared element transition.

Add the following code in the body of showLogin, before the call to addToBackStack:

```
// 1
val sharedView = findViewById<View>(R.id.logo)
// 2
addSharedElement(sharedView, sharedView.transitionName)
```

The code above does two things:

1. It gets a reference to the shared logo View. Since the Fragments are housed inside the Activity, you can use findViewById to find the view in the Fragments layout.
2. It then triggers the actual call to addSharedElement, using the shared view and its transition name (which you defined earlier).

Now, add that same code in showSignup so the shared element transition runs when the user navigates to both the login and sign-up screens:

```
val sharedView = findViewById<View>(R.id.logo)
addSharedElement(sharedView, sharedView.transitionName)
```

Finally, build and run the app. You'll see... just about nothing. Maybe a flickering Cinematic logo, if you're lucky.

What gives? It turns out you need to give the framework a few more hints about how to animate your logos.

Types of shared element transitions

You've set up your shared element transition perfectly, but you still need to tell the framework *how exactly* you want the animation to run. For example, should the size of the logo `View` on the auth `Fragment` screen grow to be the same size as the logo view on the sign-up `Fragment` screen? Should the logo `View` rotate as it moves to its final position? There are lots of questions to answer here!

To specify a `Transition` to run for the shared element transition, you'll use `sharedElementEnterTransition` on `Fragment`. Here, you can use all the `Transitions` you learned about in the previous chapter — but they won't do much.

Normally, these transitions work off of changes to a `View`'s visibility, but shared element transitions are a bit strange; one `View` isn't losing visibility as another gains visibility. The shared `View` is always visible, meaning you need a different set of `Transitions` to affect your shared element transition.

Fortunately, the Jetpack Transition library comes with several built-in `Transitions` that work specifically with shared element transitions:

- **ChangeBounds**: Animates between the layout boundaries of the two `Views`. It's so handy that you'll almost always want to reach for it because the size and/or position usually change between the two shared `Views`.
- **ChangeClipBounds**: Animates between different clip boundaries for your `View`. This is particularly helpful when you're doing a shared element transition with images.
- **ChangeImageTransform**: Animates between different `ImageView` matrices. It's critical to use this transition when doing a shared element transition with images.
- **ChangeScroll**: Animates between different scroll positions for scrollable `Views`.
- **ChangeTransform**: Animates between different rotations and scales for your `Views`. It will also do some magic around reparenting a `View` to make the animation smoother.

Now that you know the different types of `Transitions` you can use with your shared element transition, it's time to jump in and start customizing your transition.

Customizing the shared element transition

For now, you'll focus on `SignupFragment`. Later, you'll port the work you do to the `LoginFragment` to cover all your bases.

To start, you need to figure out *which* `Transitions` you want to use. The size of the logo `TextView` changes, so you'll need to use `ChangeBounds`. You'll add that transition now.

Open **SignupFragment.kt**. Add the following below the call that defines `returnTransition` in `onCreate`.:

```
sharedElementEnterTransition = ChangeBounds()
```

Build and run. You'll see an animation that looks something like this:

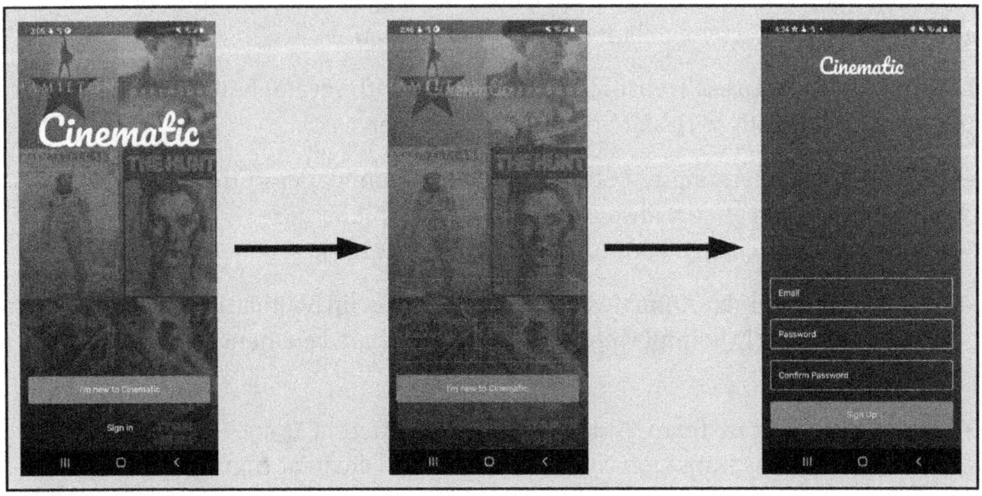

That's... interesting. It looks like the logo `TextView` fades in and out while sliding in from the side.

A couple of things are going wrong here:

1. You've included the logo `TextView` in the `MaterialSharedAxis` transition the rest of the page is using, causing it to fade in and out.
2. While the size and bounds of the logo `TextView` are animating, the actual text size isn't, making the resulting animation look wrong.

To fix the first issue, you'll use `ChangeTransform`. `ChangeTransform`'s magic reparenting logic will stop the `MaterialSharedAxis` transition from including the logo `TextView`.

Don't worry if you're confused — shared element transitions are brittle, and the `Transitions` that operate on them, like `ChangeTransform`, do many different things. No one has ever accused Google of following the single responsibility principle!

Next, you'll learn how to use `ChangeTransform` to fix the logo fading in and out.

Fixing the fading issue with ChangeTransform

For `ChangeTransform` to work, you need to use a `TransitionSet` on your `sharedElementEnterTransition`. Replace the existing `sharedElementEnterTransition` with the following:

```
// 1
val set = TransitionSet()
// 2
val changeBounds = ChangeBounds()
set.addTransition(changeBounds)

val changeTransform = ChangeTransform()
set.addTransition(changeTransform)
// 3
sharedElementEnterTransition = set
```

Here's a breakdown of the code:

1. You define a new `TransitionSet` to hold your transitions.
2. You then define a new instance of `ChangeBounds` and `ChangeTransform` and add them to the new `TransitionSet`.
3. Last but not least, you assign `set` as your `sharedElementEnterTransition`.

Adding `ChangeTransform` to the mix should pull your logo `TextView` out of the `MaterialSharedAxisTransition` animation and resolve the fading issue.

Build and run. You'll see... the same animation.

What gives? Why isn't `ChangeTransform` performing its magic to stop the `MaterialSharedAxisTransition` enter animation from including the logo `TextView`?

It turns out that `ChangeTransform` will only perform its reparenting magic *if* it detects that there's a rotation or scale change between the shared `Views`. Ideally, you'd have a `Transition` dedicated to reparenting shared `Views`. But we're not building ideal apps; we're building Android apps! And as always when building Android apps, there's a... quirky workaround you can employ to fix the issue.

Adding an invisible scale to the shared View

To fix the problem, you'll set a scale on one of the shared `Views` so there *is* a scale or rotation change, forcing `ChangeTransform` to perform the reparenting magic.

This quirky API is no match for a little creativity!

Open **fragment_auth.xml**, then add the following to the logo `TextView`:

```
android:scaleY="0.99"
```

Here, you set a `scaleY` value of `0.99`. That should be small enough that no user will notice it, while still triggering the reparenting logic.

Build and run. You'll see the following animation:

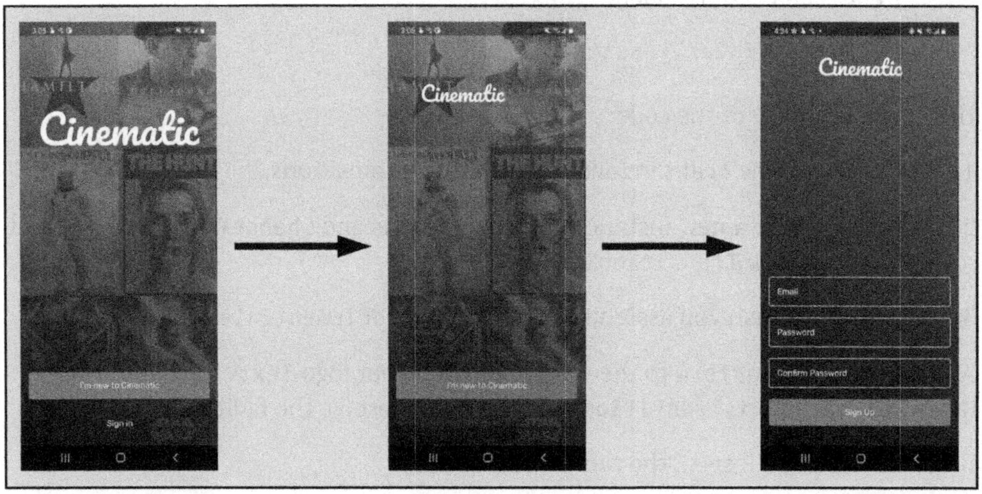

All right, you stopped the fading! Good job.

The only thing left is to have the text size animate nicely. You'll then have a full-featured shared element transition!

Creating a custom text size transition

There's good news and bad news. The bad news is that Android doesn't come with a built-in `Transition` to animate text size. The good news is — you can just make one yourself!

At its core, a `Transition` is quite simple. The abstract `Transition` class exposes a core API that you tap into to create your animations. It allows you to **capture** start and end values for the `View` you're animating via the `captureStartValues` and `captureEndValues`. You then create an `Animator` to animate the changes between those values in the `createAnimator` method. Pretty easy, right?

The starter project comes with a mostly empty shell where you'll create a fancy custom `TextSizeTransition` object. Open **TextSizeTransition.kt** and look around. There are empty stubs for `captureStartValues`, `captureEndValues`, and `createAnimator`. There's also a `companion object` with a constant `textSizeProp`. You'll use that in a moment.

You'll start by filling in `captureStartValues`.

`captureStartValues` takes one parameter: a `TransitionValues` object. `TransitionValues` is just a container for a `View` and a `HashMap` of properties. You'll store the details you care about in this object.

Speaking of details you care about, the only thing that's important here is the `textSize` of the logo `TextView`. You'll capture that now.

Add the following to the body of `captureStartValues`:

```
(transitionValues.view as? TextView)?.let { textView ->
  transitionValues.values[textSizeProp] = textView.textSize
}
```

The code above is pretty simple. It assumes you're operating on a `TextView` because using a `TextSizeTransition` on a different type of `View` doesn't make sense. It then accesses the internal `Map` of `transitionValues` and saves the `Views` `textSize` in that map, using the constant mentioned earlier as the key.

Good job, you're now saving the start values of the logo `TextView`. Next, you need to save the final values of the `TextView` in `SignupFragment`.

It turns out the `captureEndValues` code looks *exactly* like the `captureStartValues` code. To be a good programming citizen, you'll create a reusable method that you can use in both `captureStartValues` and `captureEndValues`. Add the following method below `captureEndValues`:

```
private fun captureTextSize(transitionValues: TransitionValues)
{
  (transitionValues.view as? TextView)?.let { textView ->
    transitionValues.values[TextSizeTransition.textSizeProp] =
textView.textSize
  }
}
```

Now, replace the existing body of `captureStartValues` with the following:

```
captureTextSize(transitionValues)
```

And finish by adding the same to the body of `captureEndValues`:

```
captureTextSize(transitionValues)
```

Now you're calling the newly created method in both places to avoid duplicate code.

All that's left is to write the actual animator code!

Building a text size Animator

Now that you've populated the start and end transition values, writing the actual `Animator` will be a piece of cake. All you need to do is use a `ValueAnimator` and animate between the two values!

Start by replacing the body of `createAnimator` with the following:

```
if (startValues == null || endValues == null) {
  return null
}
```

`createAnimator` provides the start and end values as parameters. If either is `null`, there's no animation to run, so simply return.

Next, you need to get the start and end values from `TransitionValues` to prepare for the actual `Animator` code. Add the following :

```
val startSize = startValues.values[textSizeProp] as Float
val endSize = endValues.values[textSizeProp] as Float
val view = endValues.view as TextView
```

Here, you pull out the start and end text sizes and declare your `View`. Since you know that this `Transition` only works with `TextViews`, you can just cast the `View` held in `endValues` to a `TextView`.

Now, it's time to return the actual animator! You'll use a `ValueAnimator` to animate between the start and end text sizes. Add the following below the declarations you just added:

```
return ValueAnimator.ofFloat(startSize, endSize).apply {
  addUpdateListener {
    view.setTextSize(TypedValue.COMPLEX_UNIT_PX,
it.animatedValue as Float)
  }
}
```

Here, you use a basic `Float` `ValueAnimator`. In the `updateListener`, you set the text sizes of your `TextView`.

And you're done! You only have a few more steps to wrap up your spiffy new animation.

Wrapping up the logo shared element transition

Now that you've created a full-fledged text size transition, it's time to see it in action.

Back in **SignupFragment.kt**, add `TextSizeTransition` to the `TransitionSet` right below the `ChangeTransform` addition:

```
val textSize = TextSizeTransition()
set.addTransition(textSize)
```

Build and run. You'll now see a beautiful shared element transition, where the root authorization screen and the sign-up screen share the logo.

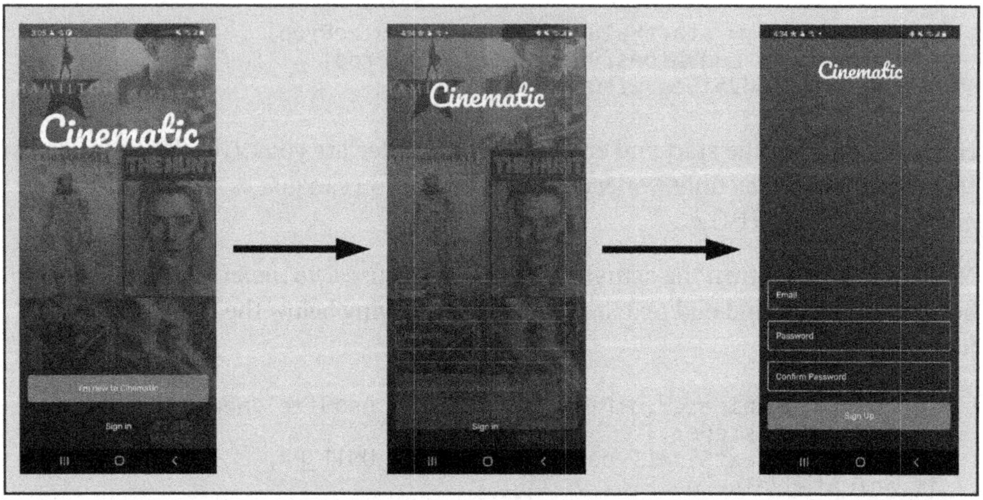

Next, you'll learn about circular reveal animations and how to use them to reveal different screens after clicking a tab!

Revealing a tab with a circular reveal

One of the coolest animations you can trigger in Android is a circular reveal animation. It's an easy way to show or hide a `View` with a circular clipping motion, adding some pizzazz to your app.

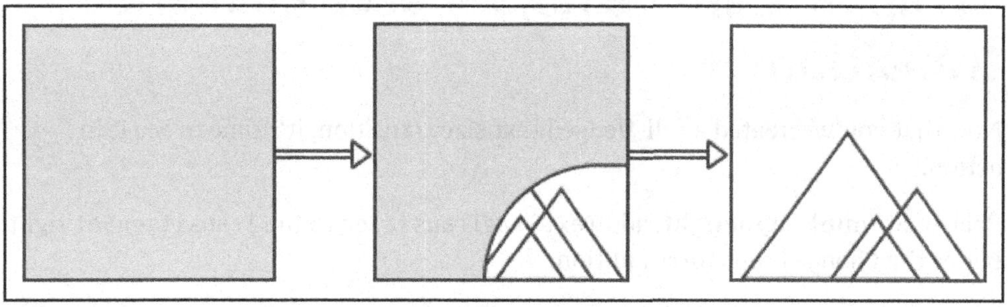

In this section, you'll learn how to use a circular reveal animation to reveal content on the main screen.

Once you're finished, tapping the **Popular** tab will reveal `PopularMoviesFragment` with a circular reveal animation that starts from the bottom-left corner of the screen, closest to the popular tab icon. Tapping the **Favorites** icon will also show a circular reveal animation starting from the bottom-right corner of the screen.

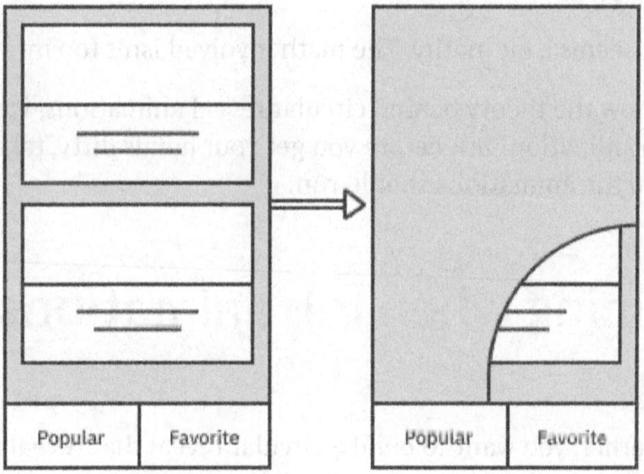

Now, it's time to learn how to construct a circular reveal animation.

Anatomy of a circular reveal

Android exposes a super convenient method, `ViewAnimationUtils.createCircularReveal`, to create the `Animator` that does the heavy lifting.

`createCircularReveal` can seem a little complicated at first, but once you break it down, it's pretty simple. It takes the following parameters:

1. **view**: The view to show or hide.
2. **centerX**: The center of the clipping circle's X coordinate — in other words, the X portion of the position that the circle should expand or contract from.
3. **centerY**: The center of the clipping circle's Y coordinate.

4. **startRadius**: The beginning radius of the clipping circle. If you try to reveal a view, the start radius would be zero because the circle is emanating out from it. When hiding a view, the start radius should be the full radius of the circle that holds the view.
5. **finalRadius**: The ending radius of the clipping circle. If you're revealing a view, that would be the radius of the circle that holds the view. If you're hiding a view, this would be zero.

Don't worry if it seems a bit mathy. The math involved isn't too intense.

Now that you know the theory behind circular reveal animations, it's time to begin building the tab animation! But before you get your hands dirty, take a moment to understand *when* the animations should run.

Determining when tab animations should run

As mentioned earlier, you want to build a circular reveal that reveals `PopularMoviesFragment` and `FavoriteMoviesFragment`. In contrast to earlier chapters, you won't use the transition framework or even `Fragment` or `Activity` animations. Instead, you'll trigger the circular reveal from within the `Fragment` at the right time.

That time is when the user taps the favorite or popular tab icons. You determined that moment in `MainActivity`. If you look in **MainActivity.kt**, you'll see some logic in the body of `navController.addOnDestinationChangedListener` that triggers when the animation should appear:

```
val shouldTriggerFavoriteAnimation = lastBackstackEntry ==
R.id.popularMoviesFragment &&
    destination.id == R.id.favoriteMoviesFragment
val shouldTriggerPopularAnimation = lastBackstackEntry ==
R.id.favoriteMoviesFragment &&
    destination.id == R.id.popularMoviesFragment

viewModel.animateFavoriteEntranceLiveData.value =
shouldTriggerFavoriteAnimation
viewModel.animatePopularEntranceLiveData.value =
shouldTriggerPopularAnimation
```

This code inspects the last-seen destination against the new destination to figure out if an animation should trigger. Moving from the popular movies screen to the favorite movies screen should trigger the favorite movies circular reveal. The opposite holds for the popular movies screen.

The code then sets a value on `MutableLiveData` in `AnimationViewModel`. The `PopularMoviesFragment` and `FavoriteMoviesFragment` screens then observe that `ViewModel`.

Open **PopularMoviesFragment.kt**. In `attachObservers`, there's a block dedicated to handling the enter animation:

```
animationViewModel.animatePopularEntranceLiveData.observe(viewLi
fecycleOwner) { shouldAnimate ->
  if (shouldAnimate) {
    animateContentIn()
  }
}
```

This block checks the `Boolean` value of the `LiveData` object and triggers `animateContentIn` when it should animate. You'll find the same structure in `FavoriteMoviesFragment`. Right now, `animateContentIn` is empty, but you'll change that shortly.

Now it's time to execute the animation!

Executing the circular reveal

Navigate to `animateContentIn` in `PopularMoviesFragment`. This is where you'll add the actual circular reveal code. You'll start by adding a `doOnPreDraw` block.

Replace the content of the method with the following:

```
binding.root.doOnPreDraw {
}
```

`doOnPreDraw` will execute an action exactly once, right before drawing the `View`. It's a handy way to ensure that the `View` is ready to be drawn before you execute an animation. You call it on the `root` of the layout binding because this animation should run on the whole layout.

Next, you'll declare some variables to use in the circular reveal. Add the following in the body of the `doOnPreDraw` block:

```
// 1
val view = binding.root
// 2
val centerX = 0
// 3
val centerY = view.height
```

In the code above, you:

1. Get a shorter reference to the `View` you're going to animate, which is the root `View` of the layout.
2. Declare the X coordinate of the center point of the clipping circle. This is the popular movies screen, so you want the circle to start from the *left* side of the screen, close to the popular icon. Therefore, you set the value to `0`.
3. Declare the Y coordinate of the center point of the clipping circle. The circle should emanate out from the bottom-left of the screen, so the Y coordinate should be the full height of the `View` — that is, at the bottom of the screen.

Next, you need to figure out what the final radius of the clipping circle should be. Add the following code after the previous declarations:

```
val finalRadius = hypot(view.width.toDouble(),
view.height.toDouble())
```

Math alert! So the clipping circle should expand to fully reveal the entire `View` of the `Fragment`. You need to figure out what the final radius of that circle should be.

The circle will expand from the bottom-left until it fills the screen. That means the *actual* circle would theoretically expand to the left and bottom, as well as to the top and right. If you imagine that full circle, the radius of it once it expands fully is the horizontal line from the bottom-left to the top-right of the screen. That line is the hypotenuse of the triangle forming the right and bottom edges of the screen, and that's where the above code comes from!

Here's a diagram to help outline the concept:

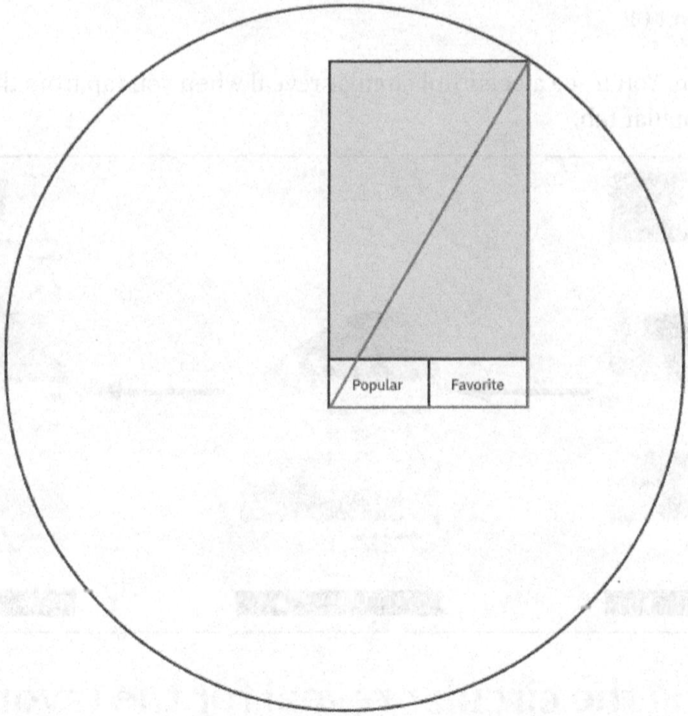

Now that all the variables are set up, it's time to create the `Animator`. Add the following after the `finalRadius` declaration:

```
val anim = ViewAnimationUtils.createCircularReveal(view,
centerX, centerY, 0f, finalRadius.toFloat())
```

Here, you use the values you defined earlier, as well as a starting radius of 0, to create the circular reveal `Animator`. Nice!

The default speed of the reveal is pretty quick, but since it's an `Animator`, you can set the duration yourself. Add the following:

```
anim.duration = 600
```

600 milliseconds looks pretty good.

Last but not least, you need to start the animation! Add one last call:

```
anim.start()
```

Build and run. You'll see a beautiful circular reveal when you tap from the favorites tab to the popular tab.

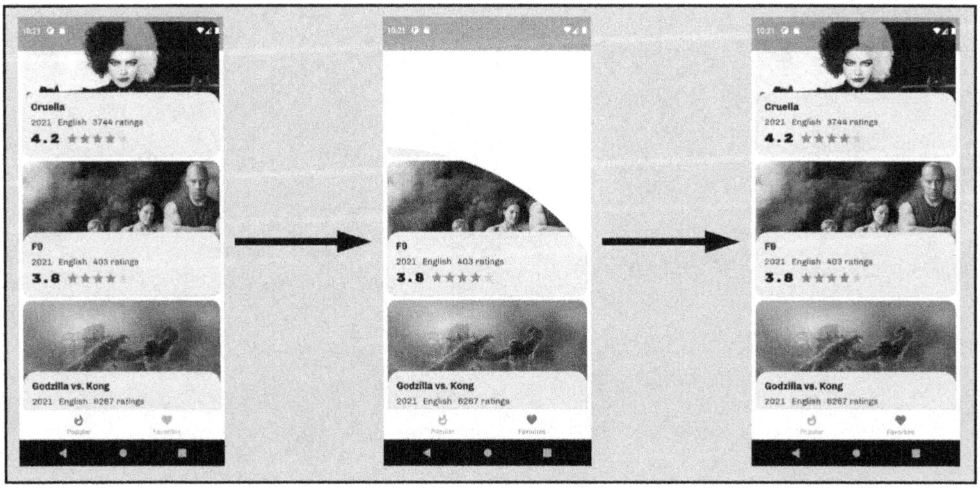

Creating the circular reveal for the favorite movies screen

All that's left now is to add very similar code to `FavoriteMoviesFragment`. Open **FavoriteMoviesFragment.kt** and replace the body of `animateContentIn` with the following:

```
binding.root.doOnPreDraw {
  val view = binding.root
  val centerX = view.width
  val centerY = view.height
  val finalRadius = hypot(view.width.toDouble(),
view.height.toDouble())
  val anim = ViewAnimationUtils.createCircularReveal(view,
centerX, centerY, 0f, finalRadius.toFloat())
  anim.duration = 600
  anim.start()
}
```

The only difference between the code above and the code you wrote previously is that you set the `centerX` value to the width of the `View` so the circular animation emanates out from the bottom *right* of the view instead of the bottom *left*.

After making sure you've marked a few movies as favorites, build and run. You'll see beautiful circular reveals for both tabs now:

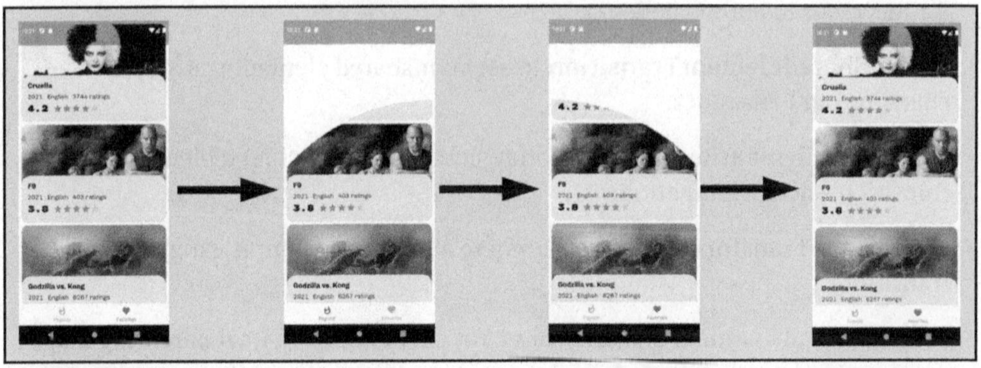

Congratulations, you've made it to the end of the screen animation section. Well done! Hopefully, you found this section enjoyable and full of great information. Along the way, you built something truly special — the Cinematic app looks beautiful and elegant, with screen animations that are not only good-looking, but also unique.

Key points

- **Shared element transitions** are a wonderful way of transitioning between screens. They improve continuity and add meaningful motion.
- To use a shared element transition, you need to define the **same transition name** for the `Views` in both `Fragments`.
- Use **setSharedElementTransition** to set your shared element transition when changing out `Fragments`.
- Use **sharedElementEnterTransition** to customize your shared element transition's actual animation.
- Use **ChangeTransform** to fix issues where a shared element is caught in another transition.
- Set a **fake scale value** if `ChangeTransform` isn't executing its reparenting magic.
- Define **custom transitions** to do things like animate text size.
- Create a **circular reveal** using `ViewAnimationUtils.createCircularReveal`.
- Use **doOnPreDraw** to execute animation code as soon as the `View` is ready to be drawn.
- Don't be afraid of using math to figure out the properties of your animations.

In the next section, you'll learn how to use list- and gesture-based animations to make your lists look equally fancy!

Section III: List & Gesture Animations

In this section you'll learn how to use another crucial type of animation for your app, List Animations and Gestures. First, you will work with basic list animations in a recyclerview. You'll use **ItemAnimator** to animate the creation, reordering and removal of items in a list. You'll use **ItemTouchHelper** animations which animate the items as the user swiptes them off or rearranges the items of a list using drag and drop gestures. You'll enable gestures on a list to detect swiping and drag and drop reording of items. You'll use **item resetting** to visually alert the user that they've swiped an item. Your app will allow users to reorder items with drag and drop in style.

You'll take a close look at how to incorporate animations while the user is scrolling items in a list. You'll set up scroll listeners, detect the scrolling gestures and how far the list has been scrolled, and respond by updating the UI when scrolling. You'll learn how to show and hide UI components when scrolling, and how to use **CoordinatorLayout** with a **CollapsingToolbarLayout** to acheive a stunning paralax effect when the user scrolls.

Chapter 7: Basic List Animations

By Filip Babić

It's hard to show everything your app offers on one static screen. Instead, most developers use a **dynamic list of data** to display items on demand — making these dynamic lists the most common UI type in mobile apps. Because they're so common, it's important to know how to animate dynamic lists.

Animating the items on the list is an opportunity to give your users useful information about what's happening with that data. For example, you can add animations when items initially appear on the screen or when they're added, moved or removed. This concept, where you use motion on the screen to give more meaning to your users' actions, is called **meaningful motion.** Whenever you add animations to your app, their purpose should always be to give the app more meaningful motion.

In this chapter, you'll learn about the animations you can apply to your list of movies. More precisely, you'll learn:

- How to write simple XML animations, then apply them to list items as **layout animations** to animate those items when they appear onscreen.
- What the `ItemAnimator` API is and how to use it to create, add, remove and move the list items' animations.
- How to use the `DiffUtil` and `ListAdapter` APIs to emit **smart data set changes**.

Now, you'll dive right in by learning about layout animations in lists!

Getting started

To begin, use Android Studio Arctic Fox or newer to open the **starter** project folder within **07-basic-list-animations** in the **aat-materials** repository. Once the project syncs, build the app. You'll see the login screen.

Layout animations

Layout animations are basic animations that run whenever you have an XML layout on the screen.

These animations only run the **first time** the `ViewGroup` appears on the screen, which makes them useful not just for list items, but also for static elements. However, because you usually show many list items, their effect is more visible in dynamic UI elements.

You'll use the same approach as you did in Chapter 1, Value & Property Animations", where you created small XML files to animate the UI.

Building layout scale animations

For your first step, you'll build a scale-up animation for your list items.

Create a new file in the **anim** package by right-clicking the **res** folder in the project structure and choosing **New ▸ Android Resource File**. For the resource type, choose **Animation** and name the file **scale_item_animation**.

Now, add the following code to the file inside the `set` tags:

```
<scale
  android:duration="500"
  android:fromXScale="0"
  android:fromYScale="0"
  android:toXScale="1"
  android:toYScale="1" />
```

In this small snippet, you've defined how the animation will behave. It will scale items up from `0` scale to `1`, making them look as if they are growing until they fill the screen. You also define the duration as `500` milliseconds, so the animation is easier to notice.

Next, create a new file in the **anim** folder called **item_animation**, using the same approach as before. Replace the emtpy `set` tags with:

```
<layoutAnimation  xmlns:android="http://schemas.android.com/apk/
res/android"
  android:animation="@anim/scale_item_animation"
  android:animationOrder="normal" />
```

In this small snippet, you've just defined a new `layoutAnimation`. You'll use the same file for all your layout animations, but you'll change the `animation` attribute to point to different animations.

`animationOrder` defines how to play the animations, in case you've defined multiple property animations in `animation`.

Now that you've defined not only the animation, but also how it will behave as a layout animation, you'll apply the result to your list items.

Open **fragment_popular.xml** and add the following line of code to `RecyclerView` underneath `android:id="@+id/popularMoviesList"`:

```
android:layoutAnimation="@anim/item_animation"
```

Using `layoutAnimation`, you define which animation will run while the UI is laid out.

Items will appear like this:

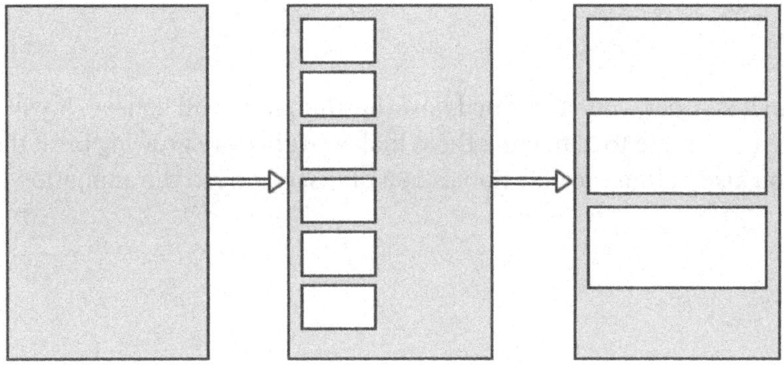

The items will be invisible at first because their scale is 0. After that, they'll slowly scale up until they reach the full scale in the UI.

Build and run. Tap **Sign In** and then tap **Login** to navigate to the popular movies. > **Note**: If using an emulator, you may have to switch to the **Favorites** tab and then back to **Popular**.

You'll now see an awesome animation when your list items appear!

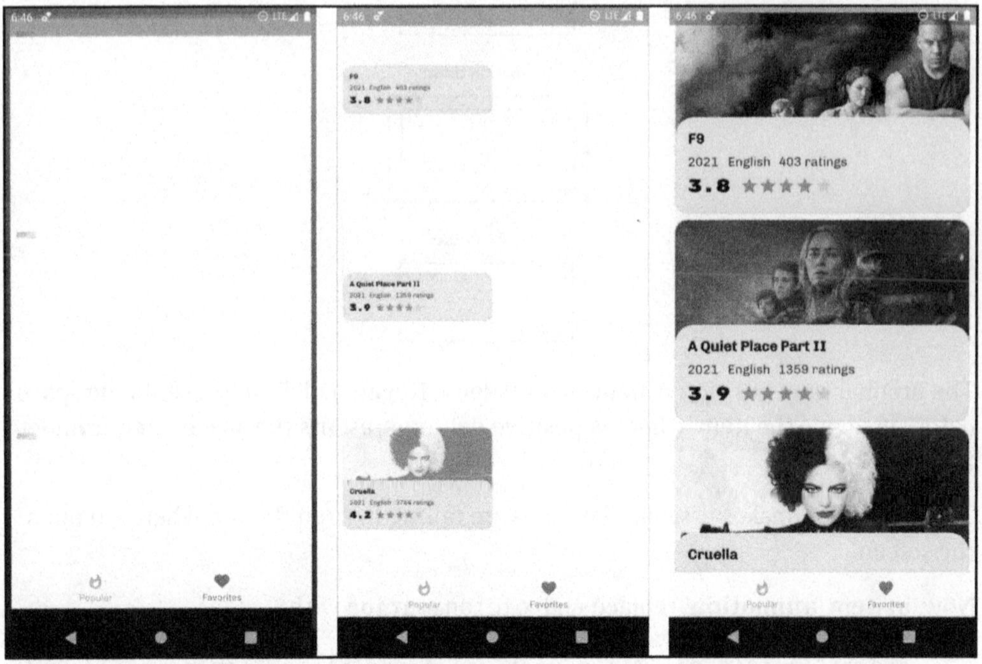

This animation not only looks nice, but it also shows users that the data they're seeing is new.

Next, you'll build a similar animation, except you'll use **translation** instead of scale.

Building translation animations

To build a translation animation, create a new file in the **anim** folder named **vertical_translation_item_animation**. Add the following code inside the `set` tags:

```
<translate
  android:duration="500"
  android:fromYDelta="-100%"
  android:toYDelta="0%" />
```

Similar to the previous animation, you define the animation's `from` and `to` values, as well as its `duration`.

The `delta` values represent the position of the item relative to the top-right corner of the screen, like so:

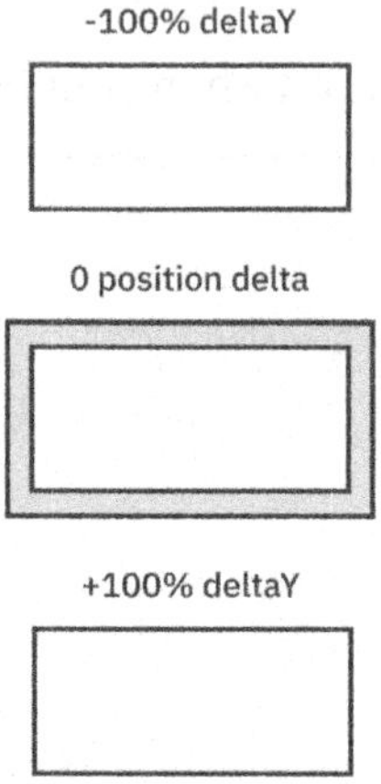

The original item position is neutral, or `0` delta. Negative delta represents the space before or above the item, whereas positive delta represents the space after or under the item.

The translation makes it seem like items are falling in from the top when you open the screen.

Now, in **item_animation**, replace `android:animation` with:

```
android:animation="@anim/vertical_translation_item_animation"
```

The code above changes the item animation to use your new translation. The animation will play out like so:

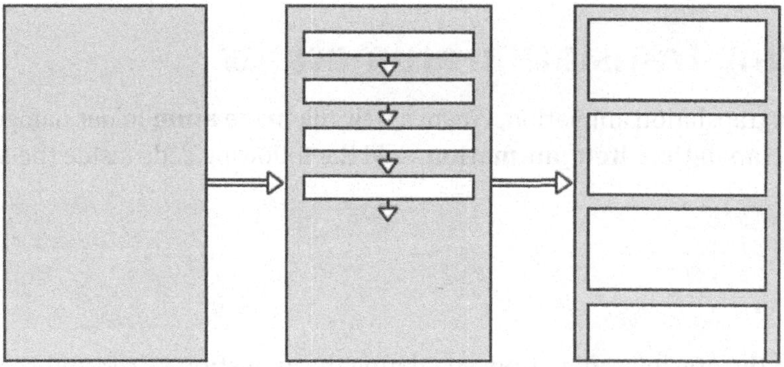

Build and run. You'll see the animation on `PopularMoviesFragment`.

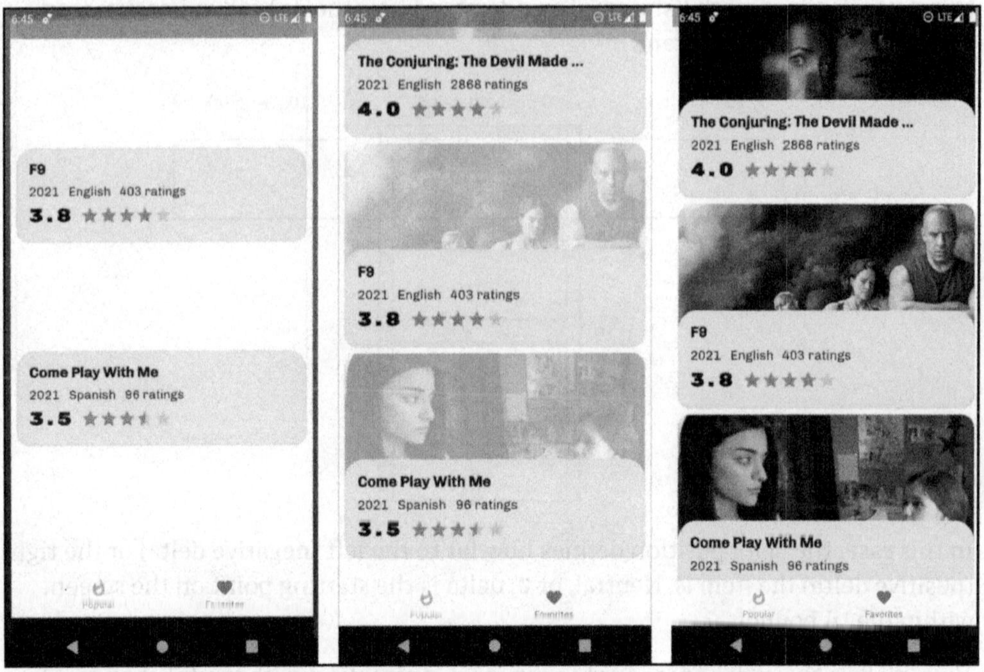

Your items act as if they're dropping into the UI from the top, which looks really cool!

Combining multiple animations

So far, with just a few lines of code, you've built two lovely animations for your list items. It's *that* easy! But it's also great to know you can apply multiple animations in your animation `set` and apply them to each list item. You'll do that next.

Create a new file in the **anim** folder called **combined_item_animation**. Add the following code inside the `set` tags:

```
<translate
  android:duration="500"
  android:fromXDelta="-100%"
  android:toXDelta="0%" />

<alpha
  android:duration="500"
  android:fromAlpha="0"
  android:toAlpha="1" />
```

Adding both of these animations to the `set` means you'll run multiple transformations on each list item. To understand how the `deltaX` animation works, look at the following diagram:

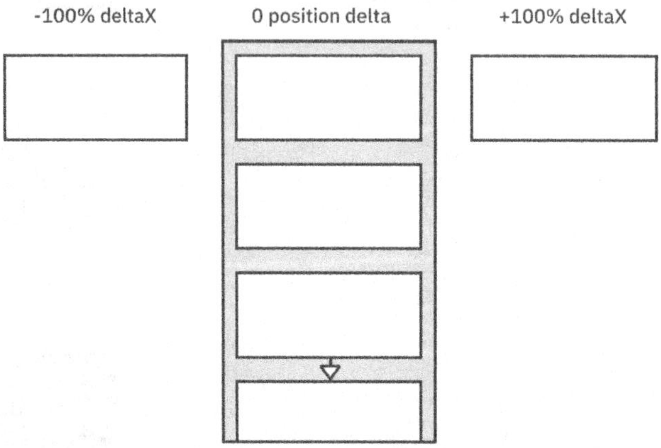

In this case, the delta position defines how far to the left (negative delta) or the right (positive delta) the item is. Neutral, or `0`, delta is the starting point on the screen, within the UI bounds.

Now, replace the `android:animation` in **item_animation** with the following:

```
android:animation="@anim/combined_item_animation"
```

You're now pointing to a different set of animations, which will apply to each of your items.

The animation will play out like this:

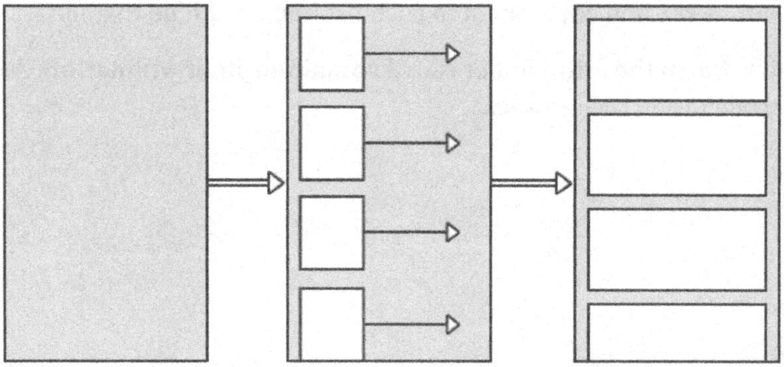

Here, the items don't just translate in horizontally with a **slide-in** animation; they also update their alpha values from fully transparent items to fully visible by using a **fade-in** animation.

Build and run. You'll see your awesome combined animation at work!

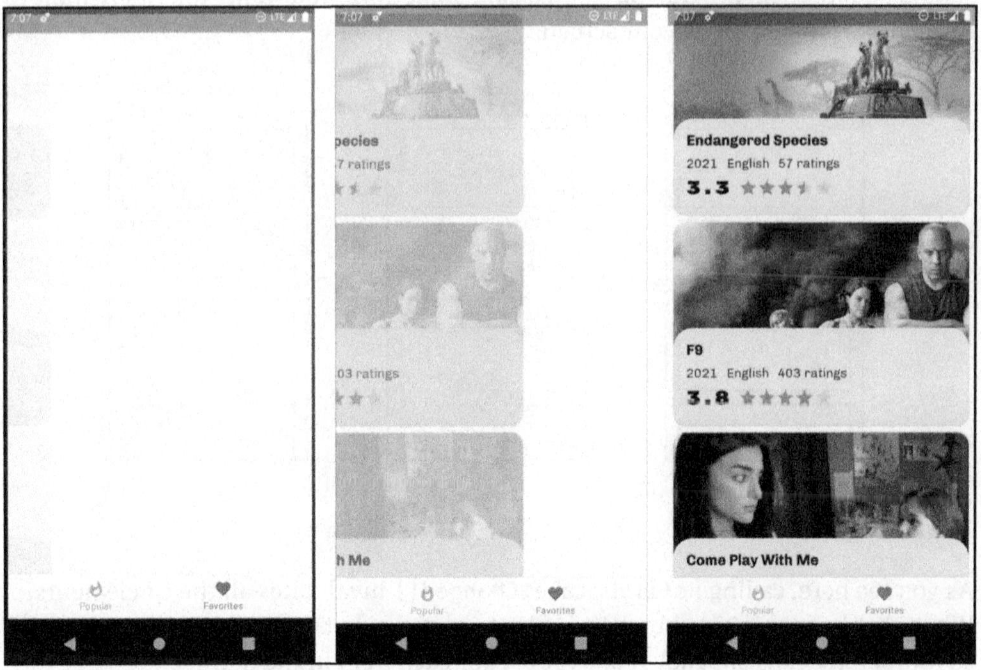

Using these basic animation types, you can achieve beautiful layout animations without much code. But these animations only occur when the items first appear.

List items are usually dynamic, which means you can add them, remove them or move them around. You'll tackle how to animate those changes next!

Using data set changes to animate list items

To animate list items when the data set changes, you'll use convenient functions in your `RecyclerViews`. Open `MoviesRecyclerAdapter` and take note of `notifyDataSetChanged()` when you call `setItems()`:

```
fun setItems(newItems: List<Movie>) {
  this.items.clear()
```

```
    this.items.addAll(newItems)
    notifyDataSetChanged() // here
  }
```

This function tells the adapter that all the items in your data set changed, so it should update them all. Obviously, this isn't something you want. You rarely want to re-render all the items on your screen.

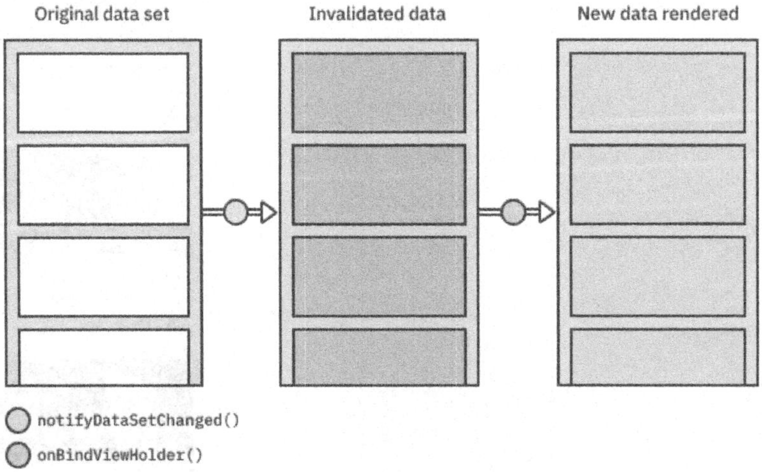

As you see here, calling `notifyDataSetChanged()` invalidates all the UI elements. When that happens, `RecyclerView.Adapter` knows that it should render new data, so it promptly calls `onBindViewHolder()` for each item in the list.

This forces it to redraw all the elements, even those that didn't change — which is an expensive operation. It's better to notify the adapter when you add or remove new items rather than invalidating everything.

Next, you'll see how to update items when you add or remove them from the list.

Removing items from the list

Open **MoviesRecyclerAdapter.kt**. You'll use this adapter to render popular movies in the `PopularMoviesFragment`. Once it's open, navigate to `onBindViewHolder()`.

Currently, you send a simple hard-coded long-tap listener within `onBindViewHolder()` to `MoviesViewHolder`:

```
override fun onBindViewHolder(holder: MoviesViewHolder,
position: Int) {
  holder.bind(items[position]) { movie ->
    this.items.remove(movie) // 1

    notifyDataSetChanged() // 2
  }
}
```

You'll use this hard-coded listener to add or remove selected items from the list, to imitate data operations. It will work like this:

1. You remove the item from `items`, which is your adapter's **data set**.
2. You need to change the `notifyDataSetChanged()` call to tell the user you removed a single item.

Change the callback you pass to `bind()` to the following:

```
holder.bind(items[position]) { movie ->
  val itemIndex = items.indexOf(movie) // 1
  this.items.remove(movie) // 2

  notifyItemRemoved(itemIndex) // 3
}
```

The snippet now does the following:

1. Fetches the index of the item you want to remove.
2. Removes the item from the list.
3. Notifies the adapter that you removed only one item at a given `itemIndex`.

This way, instead of invalidating the entire data set, you call `notifyItemRemoved()`, which tells the adapter that only one index changed and the item at the index was removed.

The animation will play out like this:

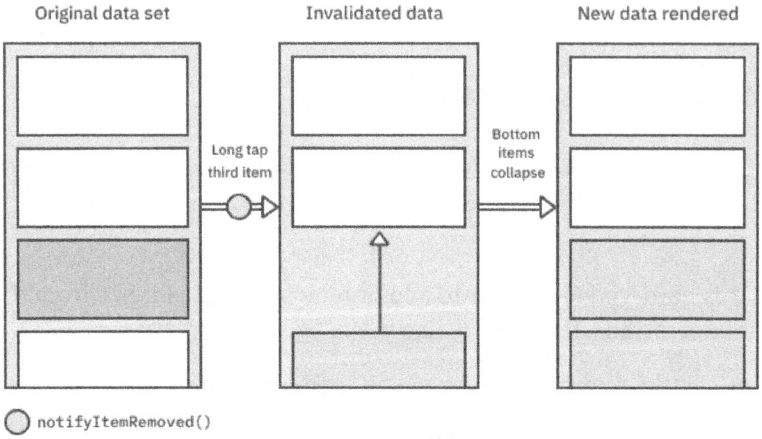

When you long-tap an item, any items below it will collapse and move up the list. This is a nice, simple animation that helps inform the users of what's happening.

Build and run. Long-tap an item in `PopularMoviesFragment`. When you remove an item, you'll now see your cool animation.

This is a good example of meaningful motion.

Next, you'll learn how to notify the adapter that you've added more items to the list.

Adding items to the list

As with `notifyItemRemoved()`, you can use `notifyItemInserted()` to tell the adapter you added new items to the list.

To do that, change the callback signature that you pass to `bind()` to:

```
holder.bind(items[position]) { movie ->
  val newIndex = (0..items.size).random() // 1
  this.items.add(newIndex, movie) // 2

  notifyItemInserted(newIndex) // 3
}
```

Instead of removing the item, you:

1. Generate a random index within the bounds of the data set.
2. Add the same item as a duplicate at the given `newIndex`.
3. Call `notifyItemInserted()` and let the adapter know that you've inserted a new item.

This time, you'll randomly add more items, which will cause other items to shift.

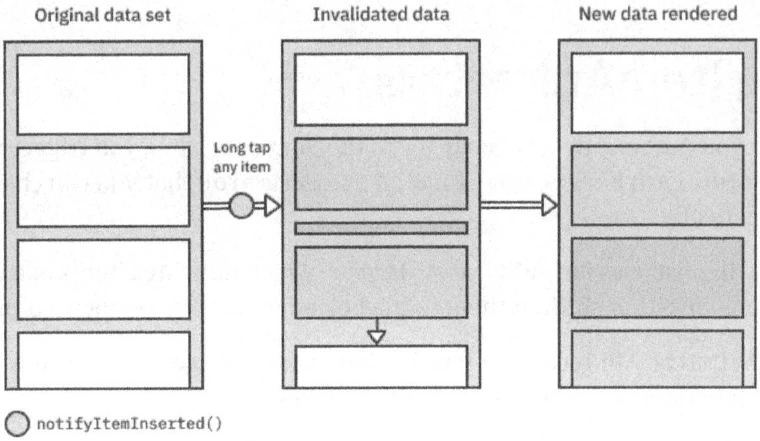

As you insert an item at a specific position, the adapter will push items underneath it to make space for the new item. This is another simple, cool animation that gives users more information about what's happening on the screen.

Build and run. You'll see the following behavior:

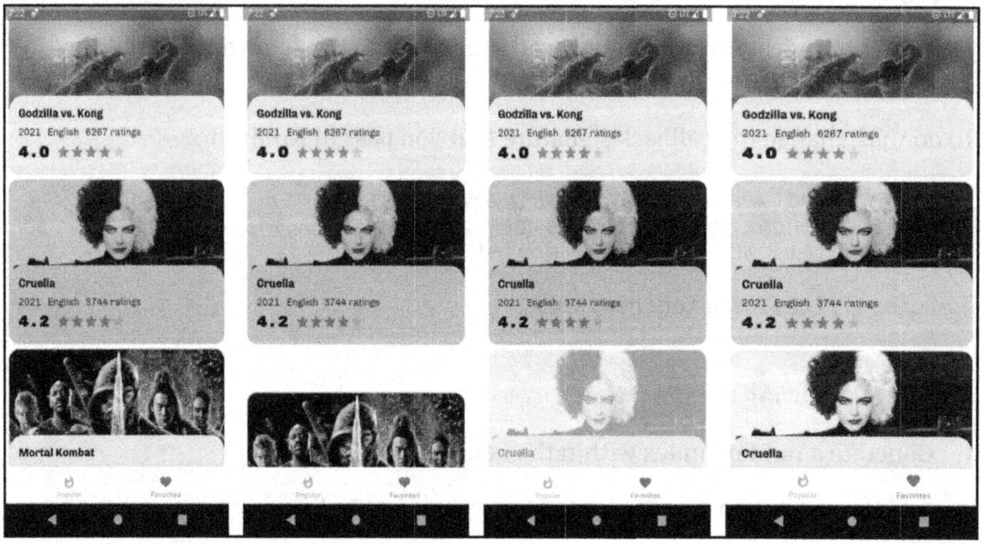

So how does the list know how to animate these items? Is there is an automatic way to notify the adapter of changes?

Well, the answer lies in a very simple API: `ItemAnimator`.

Using ItemAnimators

Whenever you post any data set changes to the `RecyclerView`, you trigger its `ItemAnimator`. Each `RecyclerView` has an `ItemAnimator` that you can change programmatically.

By default, the list uses `DefaultItemAnimator`, which animates items like you've seen so far — by either shifting them to the bottom or collapsing them to the top.

The `ItemAnimator` API receives a notification of any data set changes. It exposes four main functions to animate each type of change:

- **animateDisappearance**: Animates an item that's being removed.
- **animateAppearance**: Animates an item as it's added.

- **animatePersistance**: Runs when an item is present in the data set before and after, but the item hasn't been invalidated.
- **animateChange**: Animates an item when its position changes.

In each of these functions, the magic happens when you change something in the data set.

To override `DefaultItemAnimator`, pass in a custom instance to your `RecyclerView`, like so:

```
myRecyclerView.itemAnimator = object: RecyclerView.ItemAnimator
{
    // ... Implement your animations
}
```

`DefaultItemAnimator` is great for most applications because it supplies users with well-known behavior. However, it's worth learning how to implement a custom `ItemAnimator` so you can handle the cases where it doesn't do everything you need.

That's what you'll do next.

Creating a custom ItemAnimator

Creating custom `ItemAnimators` isn't hard. You'll learn how to do it by building a nice **scale-up** animation when you add a new item to the list.

Create a new class called `MyItemAnimator` in the `popular` package, and replace the code with the following:

```
class MyItemAnimator : DefaultItemAnimator() { // 1

  override fun animateAdd(holder: RecyclerView.ViewHolder?):
Boolean {
    if (holder != null) {
      // 2
      holder.itemView.scaleX = 0f
      holder.itemView.scaleY = 0f

      // 3
      holder.itemView.animate()
        .scaleX(1f)
        .scaleY(1f)
        .setDuration(1000)
        .start()
      return true // 4
    }
```

```
    return super.animateAdd(holder)
  }
}
```

Here's what's going on:

1. First, instead of extending from `RecyclerView.ItemAnimator`, you extend `DefaultItemAnimator()`. That way, you don't have to provide all the animations for all types of data set changes. It saves you a lot of work and gives you the ability to override only the animations you want to customize.
2. Next, since you'll be scaling items up, you set the root `View`'s `scaleX` and `scaleY` properties to `0f`, so the items don't appear on the screen.
3. You then start the animation, scaling back up to `1f`, or full item scale, for `1000` milliseconds, or one second.
4. Finally, you return `true` to tell the animator it needs to apply these animations.

It's as simple as that! Now, to apply this animator, go back to `PopularMoviesFragment` and change the following part of `onViewCreated()`:

```
binding.popularMoviesList.apply {
  adapter = popularAdapter
  itemAnimator = MyItemAnimator() // apply your animator
}
```

Finally, to make the animation more visible, change the code in `MoviesRecyclerAdapter`'s `onBindViewHolder()` to the following:

```
override fun onBindViewHolder(holder: MoviesViewHolder,
position: Int) {
  holder.bind(items[position]) { movie ->
    val newIndex = position + 1 // here
    this.items.add(newIndex, movie)

    notifyItemInserted(newIndex)
  }
}
```

Instead of using a random index to add the item, you'll just add it to the next index. That way, the animation will be easier to observe.

Build and run. You'll see the following animation:

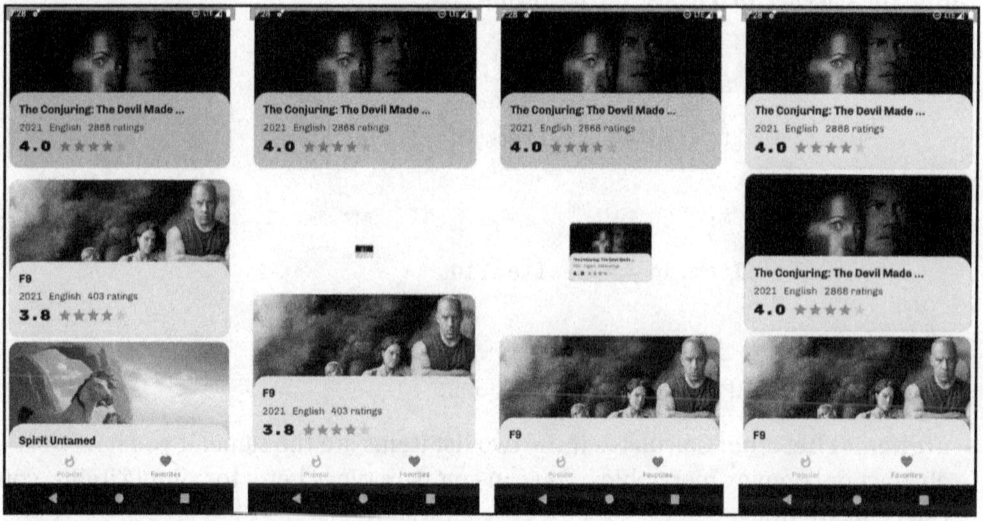

The animation looks really nice — and it was simple to implement. Remember, it's best to override `ItemAnimator` only if you can't describe your item changes with a simple shift of items. Otherwise, it might not match the behavior that Android users expect.

These animations are all simple and cool, but you have to send the updates to the adapter manually. Or do you? You'll try another way next.

DiffUtil & ListAdapter

`RecyclerView` has two APIs that help you update the items in the list automatically: `DiffUtil` and `ListAdapter`.

The `DiffUtil` API stands for **difference utility**, a class that helps you tell the difference between each item in the list when you change your data set through its `DiffUtil.ItemCallback`.

An example of `DiffUtil` implementation is `MoviesDiffCallback`. Open that file within the package **util** to see the following code:

```
class MoviesDiffCallback : DiffUtil.ItemCallback<Movie>() {
  override fun areItemsTheSame(oldItem: Movie, newItem: Movie):
Boolean {
    return oldItem.id == newItem.id
  }

  override fun areContentsTheSame(oldItem: Movie, newItem:
Movie): Boolean {
    return oldItem.id == newItem.id
  }
}
```

As you can see, the API exposes two functions:

- **areItemsTheSame**: Calculates if the two list items are the same. If you have abstract or complex hierarchies, you can compare types here; for simple items, you can compare IDs.
- **areContentsTheSame**: Calculates if the contents of the items are the same. This is useful when you have items that have many properties. That way, the item can stay the same, but its contents will change. You don't need to shift any positions, but you can update the item and reload its UI based on the new state.

In the case above, you compare the item IDs because changes in the item's ID most likely indicate that the data changed, too. And if the ID doesn't change, there won't be any new data from the API.

Pairing DiffUtil with ListAdapter

`DiffUtil` isn't very helpful on its own; it's often paired up with `ListAdapter`, another API that automates the way the adapter sends data set changes to the list.

`ListAdapter` is just an advanced `RecyclerView.Adapter` that computes data set change differences, then updates the UI efficiently because `DiffUtil`'s computations are optimized. Open **MoviesAdapter.kt** and you'll see the following signature:

```
class MoviesAdapter : ListAdapter<Movie,
MoviesAdapter.MoviesViewHolder>(MoviesDiffCallback()) { }
```

This adapter is already built for you; you'll use it to simplify the way you load and change the data set. Notice how you're passing `MoviesDiffCallback` to the constructor so it knows how to compare each item in the list.

Open **PopularMoviesFragment.kt** and near the top change the adapter to the following:

```
private val popularAdapter: MoviesAdapter by inject() //
injecting from DI
```

Instead of using the manual adapter, you use the `MoviesAdapter`. It's automated and does everything for you!

Now, also change the way you load the data at the top of `attachObservers()`:

```
private fun attachObservers() {
  viewModel.movies.observe(viewLifecycleOwner, { movies ->
    popularAdapter.submitList(movies.shuffled()) // 1

    // 2
    GlobalScope.launch {
      repeat(3) {
        delay(1000)

popularAdapter.submitList(viewModel.movies.value?.shuffled() ?:
emptyList())
      }
    }
  })
  ...
}
```

Here's what's happening in this snippet of code:

1. You set up the base use case for `movies`, calling `submitList()` whenever something changes in the database to let the adapter know about new items. Because you don't control the data in the adapter, you leave the responsibility of computing the changes to the adapter.
2. Then, you set up a fake operation within a coroutine. It delays for a second, then submits a `shuffled()` list of movies to the adapter three times. Similar to what you did when you removed or added movies to the list, this imitates data change operations.

If any of the items in your database change, they will be resubmitted, your adapter will calculate the difference using the `MoviesDiffCallback` and you'll receive an optimized, animated update.

Build and run one final time. You'll see all of your data shuffling about with a nice, animated display! Because the shuffle operations are random, it's hard to provide screenshots that showcase the behavior, so make sure to run the app!

> **Note**: This shuffle logic is great for showcasing multiple item changes, but it doesn't serve much purpose beyond that. The final project doesn't have this last change, so make sure to use the next chapter's **starter** project as you proceed through the book!

DiffUtil internals

Whenever you submit a new list to the adapter, `DiffUtil` compares all the items in the list based on the conditions in `MovieDiffCallback`.

When any positions change, `DiffUtil` lets the adapter know how to react to it depending on whether it's the same item, but it needs a data update, or if it's a completely different item needing a full update.

Internally, it triggers `ItemAnimator`, which applies whatever animations it defines for those types of changes.

It seems daunting at first, but once you realize it's only a few puzzle pieces tied together, it's simple.

Challenge: Add rotation animations

To practice using layout animations, try building a rotation animation using XML. Once you finish, apply it to your `RecyclerView` and watch your items spin around when they initially appear in the UI.

To achieve this, use the `<rotate>` animation tag and the `fromDegrees` and `toDegrees` properties to define the spin. You can also use the `pivotX` and `pivotY` properties to define the center of the rotation.

You could also combine the rotation animation with a fade-in animation to make it look even cooler.

Once you're done, be sure to check out the **challenge** project within the **07-basic-list-animations** folder, in the **aat-materials** repository, to find the solution. Compare how your animation works with the provided example.

Good luck!

Key points

- Using **layout animations**, you can apply basic animations whenever an item first appears in the list.
- Layout animations can be **translations, scaling, alpha changes** and **rotation** animations.
- You can **combine multiple simple animations** within the animation **set** to define the order they play in.
- Using data set changes, you can tell your adapters when items are removed, moved or added to the list, or which items changed their contents.
- There are various data set change functions, so be sure to use the one that best describes your change!
- To animate data changes, `RecyclerView` uses `ItemAnimator`, which exposes many functions to animate different types of changes.
- If unchanged, `RecyclerView` uses `DefaultItemAnimator`, which offers simple, predefined animations.
- You can create a custom `ItemAnimator` by extending from `DefaultItemAnimator` and overriding only the data set functions you want to change.
- If you don't want to calculate changes yourself, use the `DiffUtil` and `ListAdapter` APIs to implement automatic data changes to your list.
- When you call `submitList()` to the adapter, `DiffUtil` lets it know how to animate items.
- `DiffUtil` and `ListAdapter` use the list's `ItemAnimator` to perform required animations.
- `DiffUtil`'s computations are optimized, with most only taking **10–30 milliseconds**.

Where to go from here?

In the next chapter, you'll add more options to your list items by adding swipe gestures that let you delete items or mark them as favorites. Once you add features to update the database items, `ListAdapter` and `MovieDiffCallback` will ensure you automatically receive updates and more animations in your list.

`RecyclerView.Adapter` API gives you more options to animate data set changes. You can use the following functions to do so:

- **notifyItemChanged()**: When the item's contents change, but not its position.
- **notifyItemMoved()**: If the item's position changes, but not its content.
- **notifyItemRangeChanged()**: If multiple items in a range change.
- **notifyItemRangeInserted()**: When you insert more than one item.
- **notifyItemRangeRemoved()**: When you remove more than one item.

Try out these functions and see how the list behaves!

Alternatively, if you want to learn more about `ItemAnimators`, you can implement a custom animator that transforms each item in a custom and complex way. You can apply any animations you can think of, so go crazy!

Chapter 8: ItemTouchHelper Animations

By Filip Babić

Now that you've implemented list and layout animations, you're ready to upgrade the user experience with gestures, allowing users to swipe items off a list and rearrange them with drag and drop gestures.

In this chapter, you'll:

- Enable and recognize **gestures** in list items.
- Override **swipe** gestures to add or remove movies from favorites.
- Add **item resetting** to notify users when they've swiped an item.
- Showcase item **drag and drop** to reorder items.

You'll achieve all this using the `ItemTouchHelper` API. Next, you'll see how.

Getting started

To follow along with this chapter, open the **starter** project located in **08-itemtouchhelper-animations** within the **aat-materials** repository. This project contains your starting point for this chapter. Here, you'll add the code to build the final project of this chapter.

Once you open the project, let it sync. Then, build and run. You'll pick up where you left off in the last chapter.

Your first step toward implementing list gesture animations is to build a callback that will react to the user's gestures.

Creating ItemTouchHelper.Callback

Before you can implement gesture animations, you need to create an `ItemTouchHelper.Callback` that will enable and recognize swipe and drag-and-drop gestures.

Create a new file called **MyItemTouchHelperCallback.kt** in the **util** package. Then, add the following starting code:

```
class MyItemTouchHelperCallback(
  private val moviesRepository: MoviesRepository,
  private val lifecycleOwner: LifecycleOwner
) : ItemTouchHelper.Callback() {}
```

Your callback must extend from `ItemTouchHelper.Callback` so you can override and implement the functions that let you consume gesture events.

Notice how you also added a `moviesRepository` and a `lifecycleOwner` to the constructor. You'll use them to update the database when the user swipes movies to add or remove them from the list of favorites.

Now that you've built the base class structure, you need to override the functions that enable and react to different gestures.

First, override `getMovementFlags()` by placing the following code inside of `ItemTouchHelper.Callback`:

```
override fun getMovementFlags(
  recyclerView: RecyclerView,
  viewHolder: RecyclerView.ViewHolder
): Int {
}
```

This function is the heart of `ItemTouchHelper`. Here, you define which flags — in other words, which directions of movement for swipe and drag gestures — you want to allow on your list items.

Start by defining both the drag and swipe direction flags by inserting the following code inside `getMovementFlags`:

```
  val dragDirectionFlags = ItemTouchHelper.UP or
ItemTouchHelper.DOWN
  val swipeDirectionFlags = ItemTouchHelper.LEFT or
ItemTouchHelper.RIGHT
}
```

By combining the `ItemTouchHelper` flag constants with the `or` operator, `dragDirectionFlags` defines that the user can drag `UP` or `DOWN`. Using the same approach, `swipeDirectionFlags` defines that they can swipe `LEFT` or `RIGHT`.

These flags will unlock movement for list items when the user attempts to either swipe or drag and drop them.

Now that you've defined these flags, return them at the bottom of `getMovementFlags()`, directly below the code you added in the previous step:

```
  return makeMovementFlags(dragDirectionFlags,
swipeDirectionFlags)
```

Using `makeMovementFlags(drag, swipe)`, you return all the flags you need to enable swipe and drag gestures. Internally, `ItemTouchHelper.Callback` sets up these values so it can consume them when necessary.

At this point, you've set up the basic callback and overridden one of the methods. Before the code will compile, you'll override a few more methods to complete the callback. Your next step is to add the swipe gesture.

Adding item swipe gestures

When the user swipes an item, you'll either add or remove it from the list of favorites depending on their swipe direction. But first, you need to know which item the user selected. So your next step is to add a way to fetch the `Movie` item from the swiped `ViewHolder`.

Open `MoviesViewHolder` in `MoviesAdapter`. Above `bind` declare `movie`:

```
var movie: Movie? = null
```

This add's a new property to `MoviesViewHolder` called `movie`.

Inside of `bind` at the top, add:

```
this.movie = movie
```

You've now assigned the parameter `movie` being passed to `bind` to the new member. The result looks like:

```
inner class MoviesViewHolder(val binding: ItemMovieBinding) :
  RecyclerView.ViewHolder(binding.root) {

  var movie: Movie? = null

  fun bind(movie: Movie) {
    this.movie = movie

    ...
  }
}
```

You'll use `movie` to know which item to update in the database when the user swipes an item.

Now, go back to **MyItemTouchHelperCallback.kt** and, in `ItemTouchHelper.Callback`, override `onSwiped()` by adding the following code below `getMovementFlags`:

```
override fun onSwiped(viewHolder: RecyclerView.ViewHolder,
direction: Int) {
  val movieViewHolder = viewHolder as?
MoviesAdapter.MoviesViewHolder
  val movie = movieViewHolder?.movie
}
```

`ItemTouchHelper.Callback` triggers this function whenever the user swipes an item, so long as you've enabled the swipe gesture. In its parameters, you receive the `viewHolder` that the user swiped and the swipe `direction`. This lets you add different behavior based on those parameters, giving you a lot of control over the swipe behavior.

In the snippet above, you cast the `viewHolder` to a `MoviesAdapter.MoviesViewHolder` to fetch the movie. The next step is to check if the movie you tried to fetch exists, then update the database.

You do that by adding the next snippet of code to `onSwiped`, below the declarations you just added:

```
if (movie != null) { // 1
  val movieId = movie.id // 2
  lifecycleOwner.lifecycleScope.launch { // 3
    if (direction == ItemTouchHelper.RIGHT) { // 4
      moviesRepository.setFavorite(movieId)
    } else if (direction == ItemTouchHelper.LEFT) { // 5
      moviesRepository.removeFavorite(movieId)
    }
  }
}
```

A few things happened in this snippet:

1. You added a simple null check for `movie`. If it isn't `null`, you successfully captured the movie that's bound to the swiped item.
2. Next, you fetched the movie ID so you can update the appropriate `Movie` in the database.
3. Database operations use coroutines, so you need to launch a new coroutine using the `lifecycleOwner.lifecycleScope`.
4. If the user swiped `RIGHT`, you use `moviesRepository.setFavorite(movieId)` to add the movie to your favorites.
5. If the user swiped `LEFT`, you use `moviesRepository.removeFavorite(movieId)` to remove the movie from your favorites.

Finally, override `onMove()` by adding the following below `onSwiped`:

```
override fun onMove(
  recyclerView: RecyclerView,
  viewHolder: RecyclerView.ViewHolder,
  target: RecyclerView.ViewHolder
```

```
): Boolean {
    return false
}
```

This almost fulfills `ItemTouchHelper.Callback`'s requirements. You'll fill in the details of this function later in the chapter.

Now that you've built the animation, you need to connect the callback to your lists.

Connecting the callback to your list

Open `PopularMoviesFragment` and add the following dependency above `onCreateView()`:

```
private val moviesRepository: MoviesRepository by inject()
```

Your next goal is to use this repository to build the callback you implemented.

First, add the folowing lines of code where you set up `popularMoviesList` in `onViewCreated()`, below the existing code in `binding.popularMoviesList.apply`:

```
// 1
val itemTouchCallback =
MyItemTouchHelperCallback(moviesRepository, viewLifecycleOwner)

// 2
val itemTouchHelper = ItemTouchHelper(itemTouchCallback)

// 3
itemTouchHelper.attachToRecyclerView(this)
```

In the code above, you:

1. Use the class you implemented previously to create an instance of `ItemTouchHelper.Callback`. You pass in the repository, as well as `viewLifecycleOwner` from the `Fragment`.
2. Build a new `ItemTouchHelper`, passing in `itemTouchCallback`.
3. Attach `itemTouchHelper` to `popularMoviesList` to enable the gestures and animation logic.

Now, you need to do the same in **FavoriteMoviesFragment.kt** to make the gestures work there, too. Above `onCreateView` add:

```
private val moviesRepository: MoviesRepository by inject()
```

Then, below the existing code in `binding.favoriteMoviesList.apply`, add:

```
val itemTouchCallback =
MyItemTouchHelperCallback(moviesRepository, viewLifecycleOwner)
val itemTouchHelper = ItemTouchHelper(itemTouchCallback)
itemTouchHelper.attachToRecyclerView(this)
```

The code above creates `itemTouchCallback`, which is then passed to `ItemTouchHelper` when building `itemTouchHelper`. Finally, it attaches `itemTouchHelper` to `favoriteMoviesList`. With this, you've enabled the gestures and animation for `FavoriteMoviesFragment` as well.

Once you finish, build and run. Swipe popular movies left and right and see what happens with the list of favorites. Swiping an item left will remove it from favorites, while swiping it right will add it to the favorites.

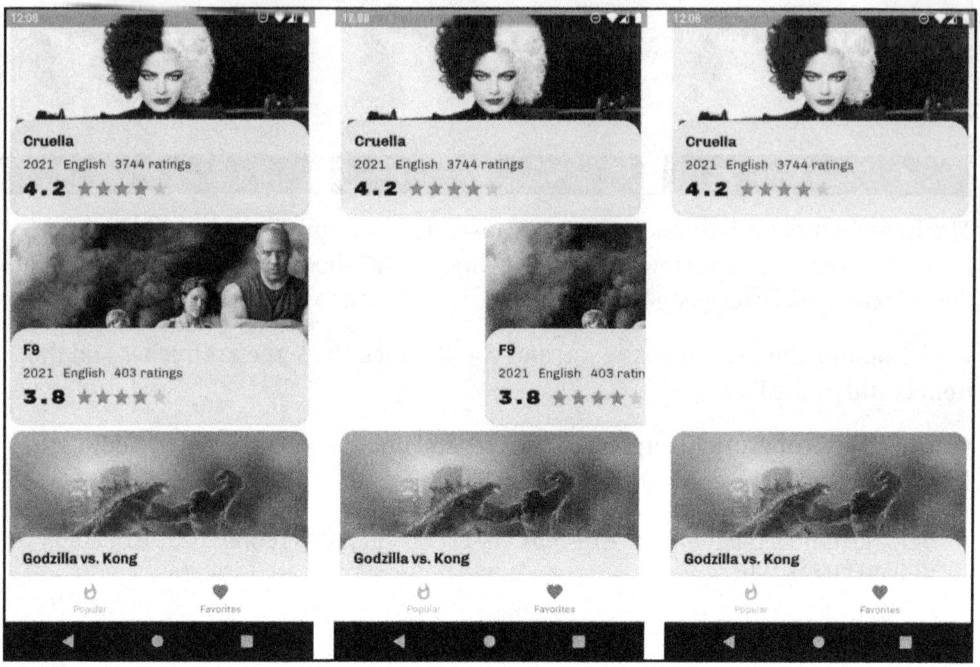

Now, you can easily add and remove movies from the favorites list in `PopularMoviesFragment`. Swiping popular movies adds them to and removes from favorites... but the movie just disappears!

Next, try swiping right on `FavoriteMoviesFragment`.

The item disappears here too! That's because the swipe gesture removes the item from the screen *visually*. However, if you swiped right, the item is still there. The data doesn't change because you haven't updated `MoviesAdapter` yet.

Click **Popular** then **Favorites** again, and you'll notice the screen refreshes and the item is still in the list.

Return to **MyItemTouchHelperCallback.kt** and update `onSwiped()` by adding the following code to the end of the function:

```
viewHolder.bindingAdapter?.notifyItemChanged(viewHolder.bindingA
dapterPosition)
```

Here, you notify the adapter that the item at the swiped position changed. The adapter knows that the user swiped the item away, so it will refresh the data and update the UI accordingly.

Build and run. Resetting will now update the items when the user swipes right on them in `FavoriteMoviesFragment`.

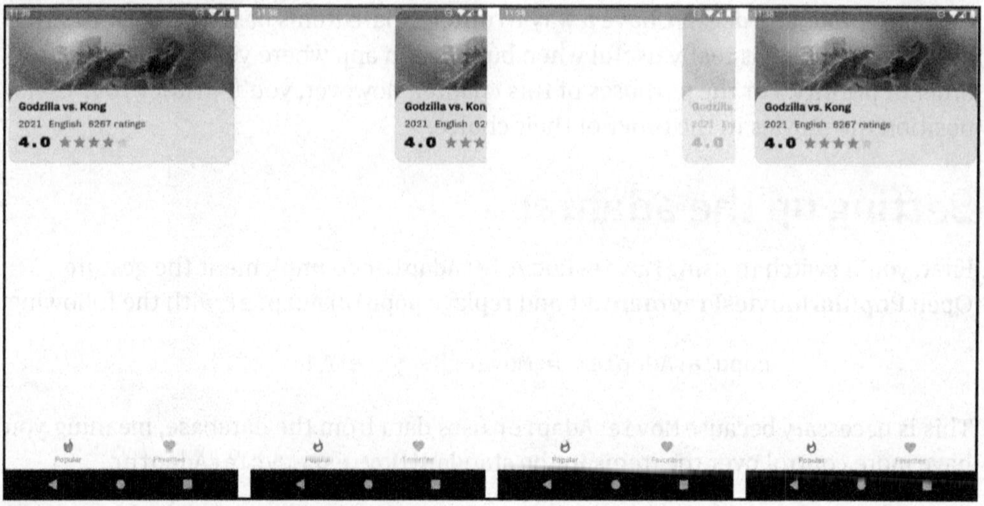

The items just reset their positions!

Item swiping is amazingly simple, yet it's powerful enough to let you create different experiences for your users, based on your app's needs. Archiving, deleting, showing menus, adding or removing favorite items and more — you can support all these different actions just with a few lines of code.

Now that you've implemented swipe gestures and animations, it's time to continue to the next way to move items: **drag and drop**.

Implementing drag-and-drop gestures

Implementing a simple drag-and-drop gesture isn't hard. However, MoviesAdapter doesn't let you make any changes to the position because it's powered by the database.

Currently, your app doesn't have a way to differentiate items based on their position in the list — which is really useful when building an app where your items have an order of priority. For the purposes of this chapter, however, you'll just let your users position the movies in the order of their choice.

Setting up the adapter

First, you'll switch to using MoviesRecyclerAdapter to implement the gesture. Open **PopularMoviesFragment.kt** and replace popularAdapter with the following:

```
private val popularAdapter = MoviesRecyclerAdapter()
```

This is necessary because MoviesAdapter uses data from the database, meaning you have more control over the items in the standard MoviesRecyclerAdapter.

Now that you've set up the adapter, you need to change MoviesViewHolder in **MoviesRecyclerAdapter.kt** to support accessing Movie, as you did previously in MoviesAdapter:

```
inner class MoviesViewHolder(val binding: ItemMovieBinding) :
  RecyclerView.ViewHolder(binding.root) {
  var movie: Movie? = null

  fun bind(movie: Movie) {
    this.movie = movie

    ...
  }
}
```

You've seen this before: You just added the option to access the Movie that's bound to the ViewHolder.

Now, add the following function to the adapter below `setItems` so you can update items while moving them around:

```
fun onItemMoved(oldPosition: Int, newPosition: Int) {
  val itemToReplace = items[oldPosition] // 1
  items.remove(itemToReplace) // 2

  val positionToMove = if (oldPosition > newPosition)
newPosition else newPosition - 1 // 3
  items.add(positionToMove, itemToReplace) // 4

  notifyItemMoved(oldPosition, positionToMove) // 5
}
```

A few things are going on here:

1. You fetch the item at its original position, which you'll replace when you finish the drag-and-drop animation.
2. You remove that item from the list; later, you'll add it back in another position.
3. You determine the item's new position. If the user moved the item up, you just swap the positions. If they move the item down, on the other hand, the position is equal to `newPosition - 1` to accommodate 0-based indices.
4. Once you know the position, you add the dragged item to the new position.
5. Finally, you update the adapter using `notifyItemMoved()`, passing in `oldPosition` and `positionToMove`.

To put it simply, you remove the item and add it either above or below its old position, based on where the user moved it. Finally, update `onBindViewHolder()` in the adapter to disable the long-tap behavior:

```
override fun onBindViewHolder(holder: MoviesViewHolder,
position: Int) {
  holder.bind(items[position]) { movie ->
    // val newIndex = position + 1
    // this.items.add(newIndex, movie)

    // notifyItemInserted(newIndex)
  }
}
```

This makes it easier to follow the drag animation when the user isn't using long taps to add new items to the list.

Moving the items

Now that you've set up the adapter and the `Fragment`, head back to `ItemTouchHelper.Callback` in **MyItemTouchHelperCallback.kt**. Check out `onMove()`:

```
override fun onMove(
  recyclerView: RecyclerView,
  viewHolder: RecyclerView.ViewHolder,
  target: RecyclerView.ViewHolder
): Boolean {
  return false
}
```

The function above notifies you when the user is dragging and moving an item in the list. This gives you access to three things: the `recyclerView` where the gesture is happening, the `viewHolder` the user is dragging and the `target`. The `target` is also a `ViewHolder`, but it represents the element you're dragging the original item *to*.

The function expects a `Boolean` that represents whether the move happened or not. In other words, it lets you know whether the items changed position.

Now, fetch the adapter from the `RecyclerView` so you can notify it of the change by replacing `return false` with the following:

```
val adapter = recyclerView.adapter as? MoviesRecyclerAdapter
```

Here, you attempt to fetch `adapter` and cast it to a `MoviesRecyclerAdapter`. If the cast succeeds, you can continue with the rest of the logic. Otherwise, `adapter` will be null.

Now that you have the adapter, you need to notify it about the move. Add the following statement right below the code you just added:

```
adapter?.onItemMoved(viewHolder.bindingAdapterPosition,
target.bindingAdapterPosition)
```

Here, you use the safe call operator and `onItemMoved()` to notify the adapter that a change took place. You get the positions from `bindingAdapterPosition`, which represents the items' positions on the list.

Finally, you need to make this function return a `Boolean`, which tells the helper whether you've successfully moved the items. In this case, `onMove` returns true whenever the adapter exists.

Now, add the next line of code below the last line you added:

```
return adapter != null
```

By returning `adapter != null` if the adapter exists, you move the items and the function returns `true`. This is a straightforward and easy way to set up `onMove()`.

Build and run. Congratulations, you can now move the items!

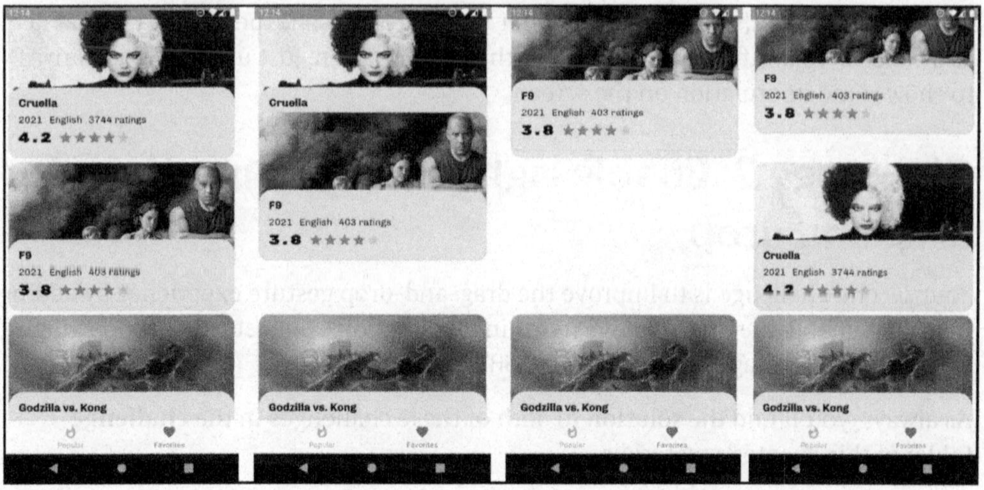

As you see, you can now drag items up and down by long-tapping on them. When you initiate the drag, you can move the item freely anywhere in the list. Once you place the item where you need it, the adapter will rearrange the data set.

It does so by using `onItemMoved()` to update the positions of the items in the list. This behavior is useful for all apps that use item ordering and priorities, such as TODO lists, sticky notes, apps with ranking systems and more.

In your example, you didn't do much with the items. Because they don't have priorities, you just changed their ordering locally. But with this knowledge, you can do so much more in your personal projects!

Challenges

Challenge 1: Add a Snackbar notification for swipes

Your first challenge is to improve the experience when swiping items by showing a `Snackbar` that gives the user more information. Your goal is to implement a notification that tells the user if they added or removed the item from the favorites list.

Here's a hint: First, add a new parameter to `MyItemTouchHelperCallback` that acts as a callback to notify your `Fragment` of the change. Then, just use the `Snackbar` API to show some information on the screen.

Challenge 2: Enable right and left directions for drag and drop

Your second challenge is to improve the drag-and-drop gesture experience by adding flags that enable the user to move items in all directions. So instead of supporting just `UP` and `DOWN` dragging, you'll add `RIGHT` and `LEFT` drag too.

As always, you'll find the solution to both of these challenges in the **challenge** folder of this chapter's materials.

Have fun! :]

Key points

- **Swipe animations** are great for adding or removing items from lists, showing extra options and showing dialogs.
- **Drag-and-drop animations** are useful for reordering items and changing their priorities.
- **ItemTouchHelper** is a simple and clean API that lets you enable and react to list item gestures.
- **ItemTouchHelper.Callback** gives you more control, while **ItemTouchHelper.SimpleCallback** offers easier implementation.
- Using **getMovementFlags()**, you define which flags the `ItemTouchHelper` API needs to consume and react to.
- To build the correct flags, use **makeMovementFlags()**.
- **onSwiped()** gives you control over what happens when you swipe items using the helper API. It exposes the swipe `direction` as well as the `ViewHolder` that you swiped.
- To handle drag-and-drop gestures, use **onMove()**.
- `onMove()` exposes the parent `RecyclerView` and the two `ViewHolders` in question. The `ViewHolders` represent the item you've moved and the position you're moving the item to.
- To integrate the `ItemTouchHelper.Callback` with your `RecyclerView`, create an **ItemTouchHelper** with the `callback` and call **itemTouchHelper.attachToRecyclerView(list)**.
- When you attach the helper to your list, it automatically **propagates the gesture events** to your callback.

Where to go from here?

`ItemTouchHelper` is easy to integrate into lists. It allows you to customize two popular types of motion in lists: swipe and drag and drop. These animations are useful when you change the state of items and data in your app. Depending on the type of app you're building, you can add many different useful features.

But `ItemTouchHelper` only allows a specific set of gestures. If you want to explore more options, you can detect gestures (https://developer.android.com/training/gestures) by using the **touch events** API. This allows you to build complex gestures and animations that support custom behavior. It lets you detect all touch events, not just swipes and long touches for dragging.

Using complex touch handling, you can build even more support for apps. For example, think about how chat apps allow you to swipe messages to select items or to show special menus.

Try building these gestures using the touch events API!

Chapter 9: Animate Scroll Gestures

By Filip Babić

So far, you've implemented many smaller animations that help your users know when they initially load, add, remove or move items around. Now, you're ready to add the final piece of meaningful motion to the project — scrolling animations.

In this chapter, you'll focus on:

- Setting up scroll listeners.
- Reading scroll gestures and the amount scrolled.
- Updating the UI when scrolling.

You'll use various APIs in this chapter, including `RecyclerView.OnScrollListener`, `CoordinatorLayout` and `CollapsingToolbarLayout`.

> **Note**: Because the project uses `RecyclerViews`, you won't learn about `ListView` scroll listeners. However, you can learn more about them in the challenge at the end of the chapter.

Scrolling animations will add a new dimension of usability to your app. Now, it's time to jump in!

Getting Started

This chapter uses some pre-baked UI code to make its setup easier, so be sure to start building it from the **starter** project. It's located in **aat-materials/09-animate-scroll-gestures**.

Once the project syncs, build and run. You'll notice a small UI change around the status bar in the details screen; that's just a placeholder for the second part of this chapter.

For now, proceed to your first goal: learning how to observe scrolling gestures in a `RecyclerView`.

Reading RecyclerView's scroll state

The first thing you'll do is add listeners to `FavoriteMoviesFragment` and `PopularMoviesFragment` — specifically, the `RecyclerView` lists.

To do that, you have to utilize the `RecyclerView.OnScrollListener` API.

Open **PopularMoviesFragment.kt**. Navigate to `onViewCreated()` and add the following piece of code inside `apply()` at the bottom, where you set up the `popularMoviesList`:

```
addOnScrollListener(object : RecyclerView.OnScrollListener() {
})
```

Here, you use `addOnScrollListener()` to add a new `OnScrollListener` to `popularMoviesList`. This allows you to start listening to scroll events and to observe the scroll state.

Now, add the following function inside `addOnScrollListener()` to start observing the scroll state:

```
override fun onScrollStateChanged(recyclerView: RecyclerView,
newState: Int) {
  super.onScrollStateChanged(recyclerView, newState)
}
```

`onScrollStateChanged()` notifies you any time the `RecyclerView` starts or stops scrolling.

You receive two parameters in the function:

- **recyclerView**: The `RecyclerView` component you're observing for scrolling gestures.
- **newState**: The new scrolling state of the list. The options are `SCROLL_STATE_IDLE`, `SCROLL_STATE_DRAGGING` or `SCROLL_STATE_SETTLING`, which represent states where the list is not moving, moving or finishing a scroll animation, respectively.

Now that you have the listener set up, you'll hook up the UI to make it change based on the scroll state.

Updating UI based on the scroll position

The observed scrolling state in `newState` will be used to determine what action to take to update the UI. Now that you're observing the scrolling state, add the following code to the function:

```
if (newState != RecyclerView.SCROLL_STATE_IDLE) {
  binding.scrollUp.hide()
} else {
  binding.scrollUp.show()
}
```

Using this small piece of code, you're reading `newState` and either showing or hiding a `FloatingActionButton` on the screen. This new button is pre-baked for you in the project. You'll use it to give the user an option to jump to the top of the list after they've scrolled down. By checking if the state is `SCROLL_STATE_IDLE` before hiding the button, you ensure the user sees it only when they stop scrolling.

Now that you've added this bit of code, open **fragment_popular.xml** and remove the `visibility` attribute from the `FloatingActionButton`. The line to remove looks like:

```
android:visibility="gone"
```

This is a very simple button that you'll use to scroll to the top. Now, build and run. You'll see the following screen:

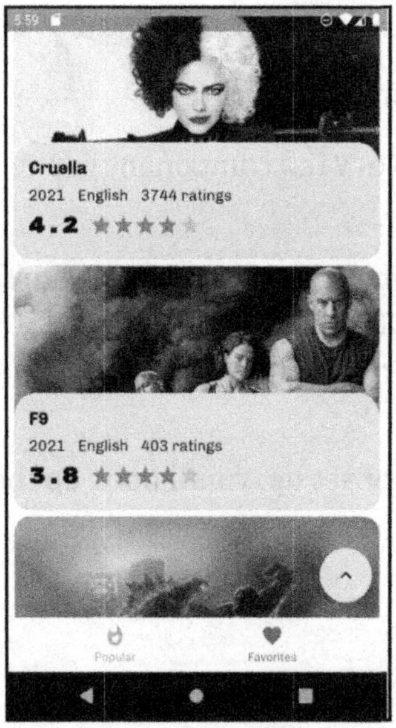

Notice that the screen how has a scroll-up `FloatingActionButton`. Try scrolling up or down, and you'll see that the `FloatingActionButton` uses a nice animation to hide itself while you're scrolling:

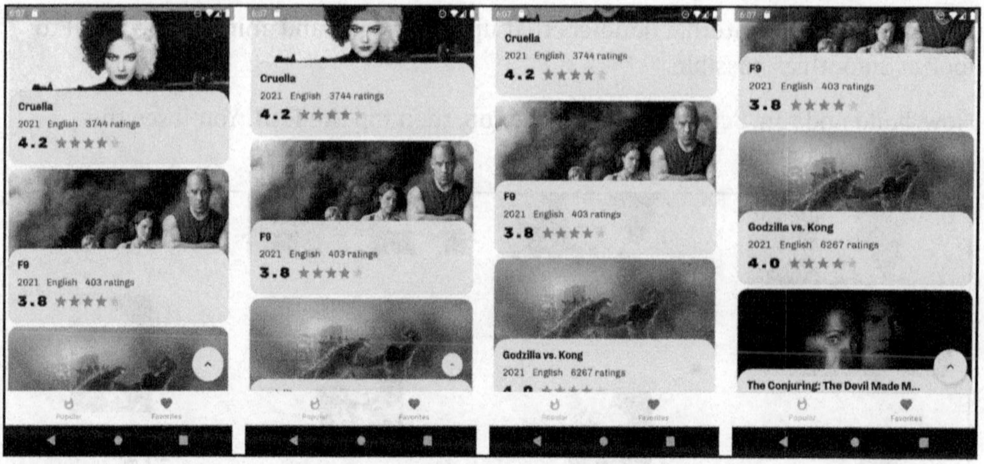

You didn't even need to do much to create that animation; you just called `show()` and `hide()`, and they took care of everything for you!

After the scrolling stops, you proceed to call `show()` — and the FAB appears again. Pretty sweet!

> **Note**: If you wanted to listen to specific scroll changes and monitor the scroll position's changes, you could also override `onScrolled()`.

There's an important problem, though — so far, the button doesn't do anything when you tap it. You'll change that next.

Animating the scroll-up FAB

The point of this FAB is to allow the user to scroll up to the start of the list. To add the functionality to the button, in **PopularMovieFragment.kt**, add the following to `scrollUp`'s `setOnClickListener()`:

```
binding.popularMoviesList.smoothScrollToPosition(0)
```

Using `smoothScrollToPosition()`, you tell the `RecyclerView` to move to a specific list item, based on its position in the list. Since you passed in `0` as the position, tapping the `scrollUp` button will bring you to the top of the list.

`RecyclerView` has internal handlers that update the list and animate the scroll to look as smooth as possible.

Now, build and run. Scroll away from the top, then tap the **FAB**. You'll see the following behavior:

When you tap the button, the list immediately starts to scroll smoothly and moves you to the top of the list. Once you reach the top of the list, the FAB animates in again; it does this because of your previous scroll implementation.

Internally, `RecyclerView` uses the `LayoutManager` API to start the scroll. This shows you how cohesive and easy to use the entire `List API` is!

An alternative to this animation is to call `recyclerView.scrollToPosition()`, which will change the list scroll state but won't animate the change.

> **Note:** `scrollUp` works well for simple scroll animations. However, if you want your animations to be more specific, to change your UI in response to specific scroll amounts or to observe pixel-perfect changes when scrolling, you can use `onScrolled()` instead. You can learn more in the official onScrolled() documentation (https://developer.android.com/reference/androidx/recyclerview/widget/RecyclerView.OnScrollListener).

Now that you've added a few simple animations to your app's scrolling and learned how to observe scrolling changes, you're ready for the next step: using complex layouts that enable scrolling animations and transformations out of the box.

You'll do that using `CoordinatorLayout`.

Building a CoordinatorLayout screen

When it comes to beautiful and meaningful animations for scrolling screens, `CoordinatorLayout` is a popular solution.

`CoordinatorLayout` is a complex layout that developers usually pair with elements like `CollapsingToolbarLayouts` and `FloatingActionButtons`. It supports complex scrolling transitions because it can propagate the scroll values to its children.

This results in built-in animations that require very little work — while being beautiful and meaningful to users.

You'll implement this in `MovieDetailsFragment` by animating the movie backdrop to have a parallax scroll animation. You'll also read the scroll value and calculate the scroll percent to apply different UI changes to the screen.

You'll start by implementing `CollapsingToolbarLayout`.

Collapsing the toolbar

To kick off the `CoordinatorLayout` setup, open **fragment_details.xml**. You'll notice `AppBarLayout` and `CollapsingToolbarLayout` at the top of the file:

```
<com.google.android.material.appbar.AppBarLayout
  android:id="@+id/app_bar"
  android:layout_width="match_parent"
  android:layout_height="wrap_content"
  android:fitsSystemWindows="true">

  <com.google.android.material.appbar.CollapsingToolbarLayout
    android:id="@+id/toolbar_layout"
    android:layout_width="match_parent"
    android:layout_height="match_parent"
    android:fitsSystemWindows="true"
    app:contentScrim="?attr/colorPrimary"
    app:layout_scrollFlags="scroll|exitUntilCollapsed"
    app:toolbarId="@+id/toolbar">

  </com.google.android.material.appbar.CollapsingToolbarLayout>

</com.google.android.material.appbar.AppBarLayout>
```

This will be the core of the layout for the scrolling animations in the `CoordinatorLayout` parent. `AppBarLayout` lets you build a top bar that reacts to scrolling gestures.

`CollapsingToolbarLayout` is a special type of a `Toolbar` that has three specific states:

- **Fully expanded**: This is the default state. It represents the UI when the screen is at the very top and the user hasn't scrolled yet.
- **Scrolled**: A middle state where the user has scrolled a certain amount, but the `Toolbar` has neither expanded nor collapsed fully.
- **Fully collapsed**: This is the state where the user has scrolled enough to fully collapse the `Toolbar`. This is an alternate state of the UI, which usually shows a part of the fully expanded UI.

Start by moving the `ImageView` with `id` of `backdrop` inside `CollapsingToolbarLayout`:

```
<com.google.android.material.appbar.CollapsingToolbarLayout
  android:id="@+id/toolbar_layout"
  android:layout_width="match_parent"
  android:layout_height="match_parent"
```

```
    android:fitsSystemWindows="true"
    app:contentScrim="?attr/colorPrimary"
    app:layout_scrollFlags="scroll|exitUntilCollapsed"
    app:toolbarId="@+id/toolbar">

    <ImageView
      android:id="@+id/backdrop"
      android:layout_width="match_parent"
      android:layout_height="300dp"
      android:scaleType="centerCrop" />

  </com.google.android.material.appbar.CollapsingToolbarLayout>
```

Also, make sure to completely remove the `MaterialCardView` with the `id` of `surface`; you won't need it anymore. The code to remove looks like:

```
  <!-- Remove this element -->
  <com.google.android.material.card.MaterialCardView
    android:id="@+id/surface"
    android:layout_width="match_parent"
    android:layout_height="600dp"
    app:cardCornerRadius="12dp"
    app:layout_constraintBottom_toBottomOf="parent"
    app:layout_constraintEnd_toEndOf="parent"
    app:layout_constraintStart_toStartOf="parent"
    app:layout_constraintTop_toBottomOf="@id/backdrop" />
```

Now that you have `backdrop` as the expanded part of the `CollapsingToolbarLayout`, you need to add a regular `Toolbar` to represent the collapsed state.

Add the following element beneath the `ImageView` with the `id` of `backdrop`:

```
  <Toolbar
    android:id="@+id/toolbar"
    android:layout_width="match_parent"
    android:layout_height="?attr/actionBarSize"
    app:layout_collapseMode="pin"/>
  </com.google.android.material.appbar.CollapsingToolbarLayout>
```

By adding `Toolbar`, you can represent some content — usually a title and action buttons — when the user scrolls away.

Notice the `layout_collapseMode` attributes on both the `backdrop` and the `toolbar`. These attributes describe how the elements should scroll and collapse in `CoordinatorLayout`.

There are three types of `collapseModes`:

- **parallax**: Use this collapse mode images. It's a well-known effect when the image moves inside the component as you scroll, causing a parallel scroll effect. It will create a nice and cool animation.
- **pin**: Use this collapse mode whenever you have elements that stick around when the `CollapsingToolbarLayout` fully collapses after a scroll. For example, you used it to keep the `Toolbar` around when the user scrolls away from the top.
- **none**: The default collapse mode, which makes the item go away completely as you scroll away from the top.

Finally, make sure to change the `ScrollView` to a `NestedScrollView`. Replace the opening `ScrollView` tag with:

```
<androidx.core.widget.NestedScrollView
  android:id="@+id/scrollView"
  android:layout_width="match_parent"
  android:layout_height="match_parent"

app:layout_behavior="com.google.android.material.appbar.AppBarLa
yout$ScrollingViewBehavior"
>
```

then replace the close tag, `</ScrollView>`, with:

```
</androidx.core.widget.NestedScrollView>
```

This is important; without it, `CoordinatorLayout` cannot process the scrolling and collapsing gestures. Also, notice the `layout_behavior` attribute — it helps `CoordinatorLayout` place the scrolling content of the screen under `AppBarLayout`, no matter how big the app bar is.

It's important to add this because `CoordinatorLayout` doesn't support ordered item placement. The way it works is similar to `FrameLayout`. It's time to render the UI!

Rendering the UI with Coordinator Layout

Now that you've set up the basic `CoordinatorLayout` and its children, open **MovieDetailsFragment.kt** add the following to the start of `renderUi()`:

```
binding.toolbar.title = movie.title
```

Here, you're adding a title to the `toolbar`, which is based on the `movie.title`. Next, remove the line of code:

```
transformations(BlurTransformation(requireContext()))
```

By removing the blur transformation, you'll show the title when the `Toolbar` collapses, and the backdrop will be clear to represent the movie image.

Now, build and run. Open the details screen to see the following behavior:

As you scroll through the details screen, the `Toolbar` collapses and the image moves with the scrolling gesture. Finally, when you reach the top, the image and the `Toolbar` crossfade so the movie title is visible.

If you try scrolling back, you'll see the animation reverse itself. This is a simple yet satisfying animation that you built without writing any animation code! How cool is that?

This animation is great for all screens where you have a lot of options or information to show to the users. You can show some information in the `Toolbar`, which you can collapse to show other UI components when the user scrolls away.

You can also react when the `Toolbar` scrolls or collapses. You'll add that feature next!

Reading CollapsingToolbarLayout scroll state

Now that you've added the basic `CollapsingToolbarLayout` implementation, it's time to improve the user experience and add more meaningful motion to the screen.

The idea is to change the UI state as you scroll, making the transition a bit nicer. As the user scrolls, you'll increase the size of the poster using `scaleX` and `scaleY`. This will give users a nicer look at the movie poster, while transitioning them into the movie's details.

To do that, you first need to read `CollapsingToolbarLayout`'s scroll state.

Open **MovieDetailsFragment.kt**. Now, add the following code inside `setupScrolling()`:

```
binding.appBar.addOnOffsetChangedListener(AppBarLayout.OnOffsetC
hangedListener { appBarLayout, verticalOffset ->
    // Update UI
  })
```

`addOnOffsetChangedListener()` allows you to bind a listener to the `appBar`, which gives you updates whenever the vertical scroll offset changes. This means you can react to user scroll gestures and tell how much the `appBar` has collapsed.

You pass in an `AppBarLayout.OnOffsetChangedListener` implementation, which gives you access to two properties:

- **appBarLayout**: The `appBar` that's being scrolled and collapsed.
- **verticalOffset**: How far the `appBar` has already collapsed, in pixels.

Using these two properties, you can figure out what percentage of the `CollapsingToolbarLayout` has collapsed and react by applying different UI changes to the rest of your UI.

You'll do that next.

Calculating how much the toolbar has collapsed

To calculate the collapse percentage, add the following code inside the listener you just added:

```
val scrollRange = appBarLayout.totalScrollRange.toFloat()
val scrollPercent = abs(verticalOffset / scrollRange)
```

Using `appBarLayout`, you can calculate the `totalScrollRange` of the `CollapsingToolbarLayout` — in other words, how much you have to scroll to fully collapse the `Toolbar`. Once you have that, you can calculate the `scrollPercent` by dividing the `verticalOffset` by the `scrollRange`.

Next, below the code you just added, add the logic to increase the `scale` of the movie poster:

```
val scale = (1 + scrollPercent)
binding.posterContainer.scaleX = scale
binding.posterContainer.scaleY = scale
```

By adding up `1` and `scrollPercent`, you'll change the scale of the movie poster from `1.0` to `2.0`, making it twice the scale when you fully collapse the toolbar. Once you apply that scale to the `posterContainer`, it'll change in size as you scroll.

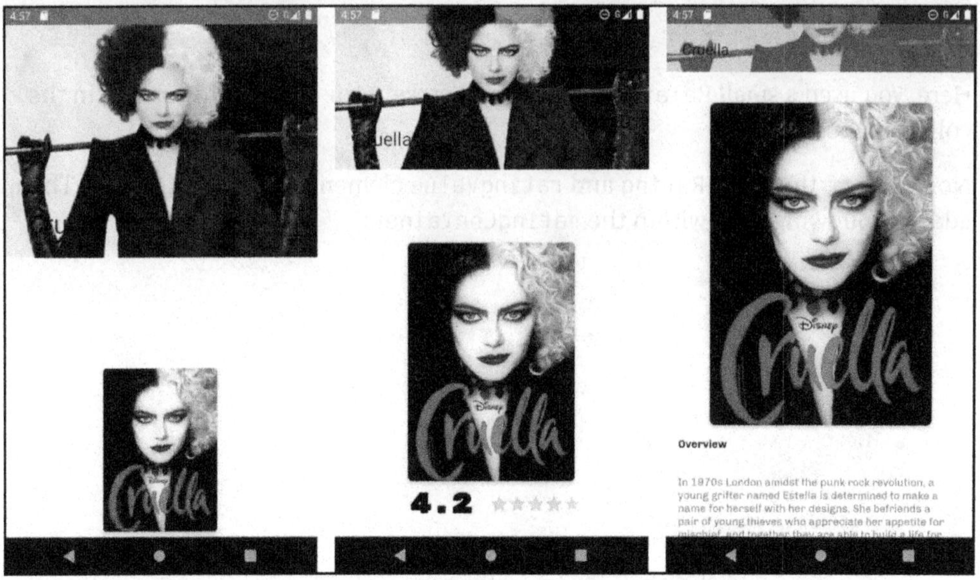

As you scroll down to the movie details, the poster scales up. This gives the details screen a nice look and feel — you get to see the poster while you browse through the information. Then, as you go back, the poster scales down and the toolbar expands, giving you a nice transition effect.

Your animations are really starting to shape up, but there are still a few points where you can polish them even more. For example, when the poster scales, it covers up the movie rating.

To fix this, you'll move the movie rating to the header when the toolbar collapses.

Adding custom Toolbar content

To improve the animation behavior, open **fragment_details.xml**.

Head to the `CollapsingToolbarLayout` element and add the following code underneath the `Toolbar`:

```
<RelativeLayout
  android:id="@+id/ratingContainer"
  android:layout_width="match_parent"
  android:alpha="0"
  android:layout_height="?attr/actionBarSize"
  android:layout_gravity="bottom|end|center_vertical"
  app:layout_collapseMode="pin"
  app:layout_scrollFlags="scroll|exitUntilCollapsed|snap">

</RelativeLayout>
```

Here, you used a small `RelativeLayout` to represent the rating information in the collapsing toolbar.

Now, remove the `movieRating` and `ratingValue` elements from the XML file. Then, add the following code within the `ratingContainer`:

```
<RatingBar
  android:id="@+id/movieRating"
  style="@style/Widget.AppCompat.RatingBar.Small"
  android:layout_width="wrap_content"
  android:layout_height="wrap_content"
  android:layout_centerVertical="true"
  android:layout_margin="16dp"
  android:layout_toStartOf="@id/ratingValue"
  android:elevation="4dp"
  android:isIndicator="true"
  android:numStars="5"
  android:progressTint="@color/colorRating"
  android:rating="3.5"
```

```
    android:scaleX="1.5"
    android:scaleY="1.5" />

  <TextView
    android:id="@+id/ratingValue"
    android:layout_width="wrap_content"
    android:layout_height="wrap_content"
    android:layout_alignParentEnd="true"
    android:layout_centerVertical="true"
    android:layout_marginStart="16dp"
    android:layout_marginEnd="16dp"
    android:elevation="4dp"
    android:fontFamily="@font/rubik_one"
    android:letterSpacing="-0.1"
    android:textColor="?colorOnPrimary"
    android:textSize="32sp"
    android:textStyle="bold"
    tools:text="4.2" />
```

These two elements are similar to what you used before, just written in a way that works with `RelativeLayout`.

Now, also make sure to update the `elevation` in `posterContainer` to 24dp so it looks like:

```
android:elevation="24dp"
```

This increases the elevation of `posterContainer`. Then update `app:layout_constraintTop_toBottomOf` in `overviewHeader` to `@id/posterContainer`:

```
    app:layout_constraintTop_toBottomOf="@id/posterContainer"
```

This will fix the constraints after you moved `ratingValue` and `movieRating` into `ratingContainer`.

Now that you've fixed the constraints and moved the rating information to the collapsible header, it's time to make the container fade in as you scroll.

Adding a fade-in animation to the container

Open **MovieDetailsFragment.kt** and navigate to `setupScrolling()`.

Add the following code at the end of the offset listener:

```
binding.ratingContainer.alpha = scrollPercent
```

Using this code, you'll slowly fade in the rating information. This will prevent the rating information from covering up the image when the `Toolbar` is expanded.

Now, build and run. You'll see the movie rating slowly fade in as you scroll and collapse the toolbar.

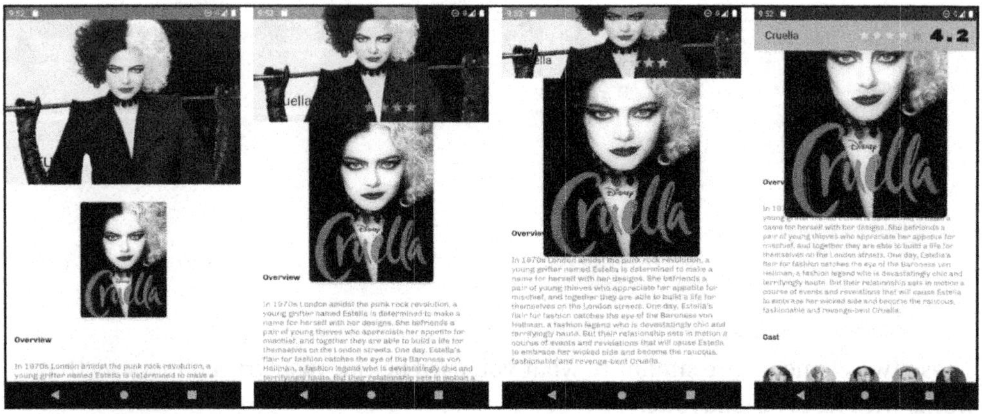

In the meantime, the poster will scale up and take over more space so you can still look at the image of the movie when you scroll.

Improving the poster scale animation

Now that you've set up the rating, it's time to make the poster scale animation even nicer. Right now, it covers the rest of the UI as it scales up. Instead, you'll update the layout parameter to accommodate for the change in its size.

Find the following properties at the top of the class:

```
private var originalWidth by Delegates.notNull<Int>()
private var originalHeight by Delegates.notNull<Int>()
```

and replace them with:

```
private var originalWidth: Int = 0
private var originalHeight: Int = 0
```

These two properties represent posterContainer's original width and height. You'll use them to remember what the original size was and to scale up from there as you scroll.

Now, add the following code at the bottom of onViewCreated():

```
binding.posterContainer.doOnLayout {
  originalWidth = it.width
  originalHeight = it.height
}
```

Using doOnLayout(), you tell the View to perform an action when the system lays out the movie poster and draws it. This way, you can get the correct size of the container. You'll use that value to scale the container as you scroll.

Next, to apply the animation to posterContainer as you scroll and collapse the Toolbar, remove the following lines from setupScrolling():

```
binding.posterContainer.scaleX = scale
binding.posterContainer.scaleY = scale
```

and replace them with the following:

```
binding.posterContainer.updateLayoutParams {
  this.width = (scale * originalWidth).toInt()
  this.height = (scale * originalHeight).toInt()
}
```

Instead of applying a scaleX or scaleY animation, you now change its width and height. You used updateLayoutParams() and the originalWidth and originalHeight properties to do this.

This function lets you update and change the parameters that calculate the size of the View. Using scale * originalWidth and setting the scale to (1 + scrollPercent), you change the size of the posterContainer from a scale of 1.0 to a scale of 2.0. This is similar to what you did before when calculating the scale.

The difference is that, this time, the size changes instead of the scale. The result is that the View won't cover up other elements.

Removing the empty space.

Build and run. At this point, you might notice that there's quite a bit of empty space at the top of the poster. You'll fix this next.

Open **fragment_details.xml** and change the `posterContainer`'s `marginTop` to `32dp`:

```
android:layout_marginTop="32dp"
```

With this change, you'll see there's not so much empty space at the top of the poster.

Build and run one final time. You'll see the poster increase in size.

Congratulations, everything works smoothly now!

This is now a much better animation. There's no item overlap, and everything looks cohesive and clean! If you start scrolling back and expanding the `Toolbar`, `posterContainer` will reduce in size and slowly go back to the `1.0` scale — its original size.

The animation will look like this:

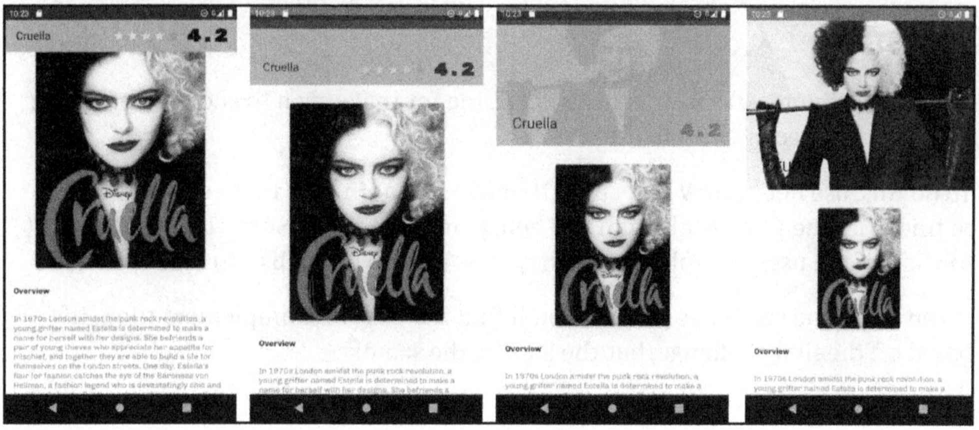

Pretty cool... and all with just a few lines of code! You're now ready to apply beautiful and simple animations to lists and scrollable screens in your apps. :]

Challenges

Challenge 1: Build a ListView and its scroll listener

In this challenge, you'll learn how to use the `ListView` API to achieve the same scrolling behavior as with the `RecyclerView`.

You need to implement a `ListView` and an adapter as a `BaseAdapter`. Once you do that, make sure to fill the adapter with the movie data and to connect an `OnScrollListener` to it. That performs the same FAB show-and-hide logic.

Check out the challenge projects to find the solution!

Challenge 2: Use scroll listeners to show and hide the FAB

Try to implement extra logic for the `FloatingActionButton` to show it only when the list is scrolled away from the top.

To do this, use `RecyclerView.LayoutManager.findFirstVisibleItemPosition()` to find what the first visible item is. Then, pair it up with `onScrollStateChanged()` to check if the user is scrolling or if they're at the top of the list, to hide the FAB.

If you check the challenge project, you'll find the `ListView` implementation. It's based off the first challenge, but the logic is the same!

Key points

- When using ScrollViews, you can control scrolling gestures and animations using the ListView's OnScrollListener, the RecyclerView.OnScrollListener, a CoordinatorLayout and a View.OnScrollChangeListener.
- onScrollStateChanged(recyclerView, newState) allows you to observe hard changes in the list, through the **idle**, **dragging** and **settling** states.
- Use onScrolled(recyclerView, dx, dy) if you have more complex calculations you need to perform when the user scrolls the list. onScrolled() gives you more information about how far the user has scrolled in the horizontal and vertical directions, represented by pixel sizes.
- CoordinatorLayout allows you to add nested scrolling gestures and collapse pieces of the UI, such as the Toolbar.
- Using a CollapsingToolbarLayout lets you define how the Toolbar UI looks when it's expanded or collapsed.
- Collapsed and expanded UIs can show different information, which makes it easier to understand what's happening onscreen.
- Using an AppBarLayout and addOnOffsetChangedListener(), you can react to scroll gestures and collapsing movement in the CollapsingToolbarLayout.
- AppBarLayout.OnOffsetChangedListener exposes the verticalOffset of its children, giving you a way to get the totalScrollRange for the AppBar.
- Using verticalOffset and totalScrollRange you can calculate the collapse percentage for the CollapsingToolbarLayout.
- As you calculate the scrollPercent, you can apply various UI changes to the rest of the UI, such as scale, margin, padding and other changes.
- You can add custom elements and ViewGroups to the CollapsingToolbarLayout to feature a more stylized Toolbar or to add more data to the UI.
- The Toolbar can do more than just show a title. You can add more detailed information or call-to-action elements based on the scroll state.
- Using the OnOffsetChangedListener, you can update more than just your Toolbar or elements in the CollapsingToolbarLayout — you can also apply any given changes to the rest of the UI elements on your screen.

Where to go from here?

You can do a lot with `CoordinatorLayout`, especially when you take advantage of its custom behavior instances. If you want to learn more about the features that the `CoordinatorLayout` supports, check out the official CoordinatorLayout documentation (https://developer.android.com/reference/androidx/coordinatorlayout/widget/CoordinatorLayout).

You can also check out the CoordinatorLayout.Behavior documentation (https://developer.android.com/reference/androidx/coordinatorlayout/widget/CoordinatorLayout.Behavior) if you need to customize what happens to elements and how they move around when you scroll.

Finally, make sure to check out the official Android Developers' blog post (https://medium.com/androiddevelopers/intercepting-everything-with-coordinatorlayout-behaviors-8c6adc140c26) about intercepting events with the `CoordinatorLayout`.

Now that you've learned all about various scrolling and list item animations, you're ready to serve data to your users with a bit of style! List and scrolling animations are the most common type of animations in apps, because a core feature of most apps is presenting specific types of data and allowing different actions based on that data.

This can be anything from **creating**, **reading**, **updating** and **deleting** data — also known as CRUD operations — or simply browsing through catered content such as movies, user and news posts, images and videos.

Whatever your use case, your users are likely to scroll through a bunch of data and apply some operations to it, so be sure to arm your apps with meaningful scrolling and list item animations to make the experience more enjoyable.

If you're looking for inspiration for what you can do with list items and scrolling, be sure to check out Dribble (https://dribbble.com/search/scroll). It offers many examples of animations and meaningful motion, especially in modern apps!

Section IV: Jetpack Compose Animations

This will take you through an overview of Jetpack Compose animations. You'll use AnimatedVisibilty to look at the state and determine the visibility of the Composables wrapped within it. You'll learn how to use different types of animations like slide-in or fade-in, and how to apply multiple animations at a time. You'll also learn about animating the properties of views such as size or color, and how to animate the state changes in your app.

Chapter 10: Jetpack Compose Animations

By Prateek Prasad

So far in this book, you've worked on animating views and screens based on the UI toolkit. However, now that Jetpack Compose is gaining in popularity, more and more apps will start migrating to it, so it's a good idea to know how to animate those apps.

Jetpack Compose offers a host of modern features when building UIs, and it makes things like state management a lot simpler. In this chapter, you'll learn about animations in Jetpack Compose.

Setting up the project

Open the starter project for this chapter in Android Studio. Build and run. You'll notice that everything looks the same as in the previous chapter.

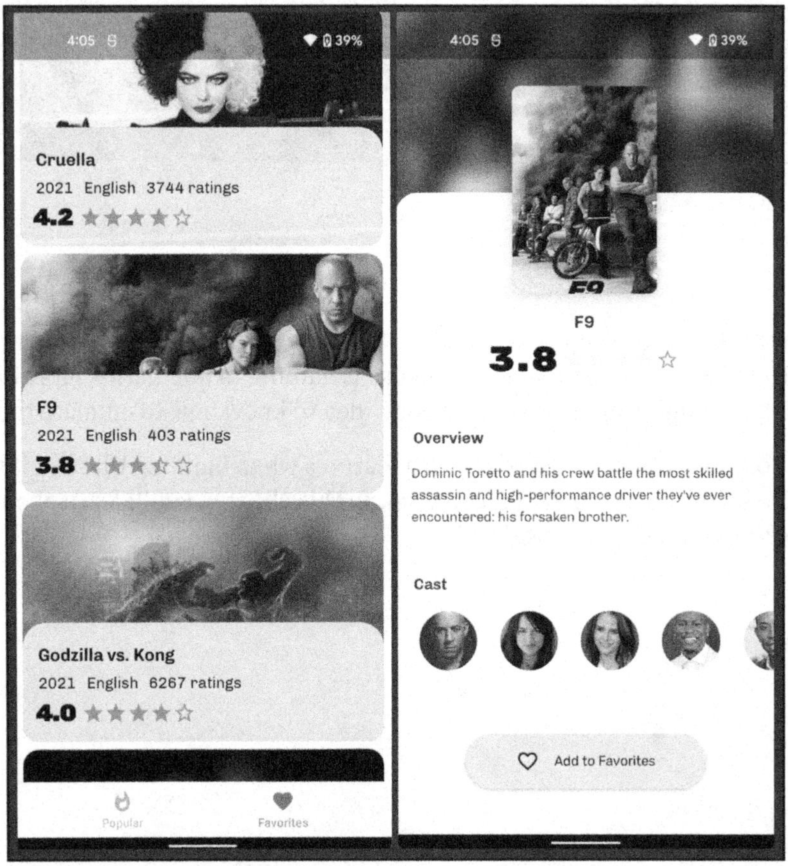

The difference lies in the project's code.

Expand the project structure, and you'll notice a new package named **ui**:

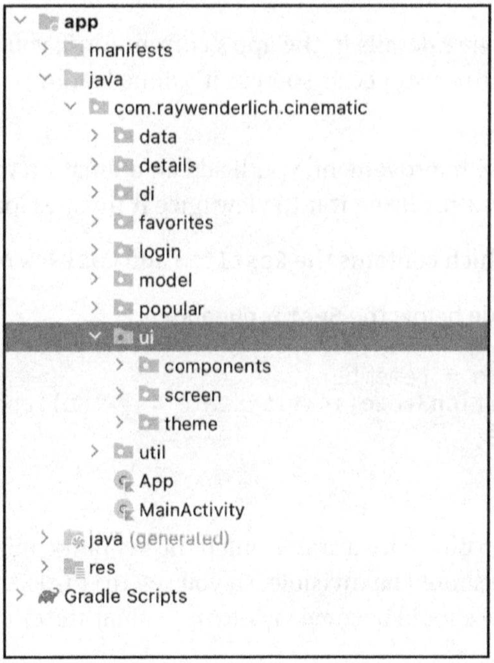

The UI package contains three packages:

- **components**: Contains the components built using Jetpack Compose.
- **screen**: Contains the screens built using Jetpack Compose and the components mentioned above.
- **theme**: Contains the color and typography definition used to build the theme for the app.

The rest of the core architecture of the app is still the same, down to the UI scaffold. The three screens of your app still use fragments, but the fragments host composable functions instead of inflating an XML.

With that out of the way, you'll now dive in and add some sweet animations to this app.

Animating visibility changes

When you open a movie's details in the app's current form, you'll notice that the **Cast** section snaps into existence as soon as it's done loading — which feels quite janky.

For your first bit of UX improvement, you'll add an animation that animates the cast row's visibility to smoothly bring it into view once it finishes loading.

Open **CastRow.kt**, which contains the `CastItem` and `CastRow` composable functions.

Add the following code below the `SectionHeader`:

```
val visibleState = remember {
  MutableTransitionState(initialState = false).apply {
    targetState = true
  }
}
```

In the snippet above, you create a state, which the visibility animation will use. Initially, the cast row should be invisible, so you set `initialState` to **false**. However, the cast row should become visible in its final state, so you set the `targetState` to **true**.

Next, wrap the `LazyRow` inside an `AnimatedVisibility` composable:

```
AnimatedVisibility(
  visibleState = visibileState,
  enter = fadeIn()
) {
  LazyRow(contentPadding = PaddingValues(end = 24.dp)) {
    items(it) {
      CastItem(it.profilePath)
    }
  }
}
```

`AnimatedVisibility` takes in a state to determine the visibility of its wrapped composable. It also accepts an enter and exit transition for the animation. In this case, you use a `fadeIn` enter transition.

Before you build and run the app to check out the animation, there's one small step you need to take: As of this writing, `AnimatedVisibility` is still an experimental animation API. So you need to annotate the composable functions using `AnimatedVisibility` with an `@ExperimentalAnimationApi` annotation.

You need to do the same for any component that might end up using a composable that uses `AnimatedVisibility`.

Add the annotation above the `CastRow` as shown below.

```
@ExperimentalAnimationApi
@Composable
fun CastRow(cast: List<Cast>?) {
    ...
}
```

Repeat the same step as above and add the `@ExperimentalAnimationApi` for the `MovieDetails`, `MovieDetailsBody` and `MovieDetailsContent` composable functions located in **MovieDetails.kt**.

Wasn't that fun!

Now, build and run. When you tap any movie to bring up the details screen, you'll notice that the cast row subtly fades into view.

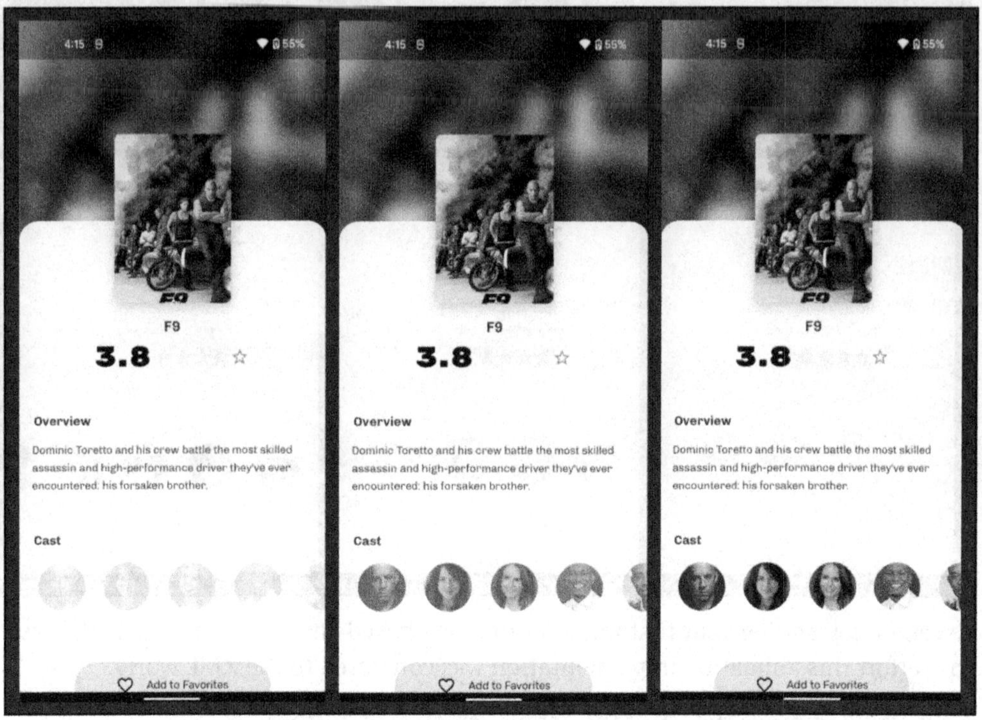

While the fade-in animation is pretty fun now, there's still room to spice it up a bit.

Adding a slide-in animation

To make your animation a little more exciting, you'll now introduce a slide-in animation when the cast row appears.

Open **CastRow.kt** and chain a `slideInVertically()` animation to `AnimatedVisibility`'s enter animation, in `CastRow` as shown below:

```
enter = fadeIn() + slideInVertically()
```

`AnimatedVisibility` allows you to chain multiple animations together in sequence using the + operator.

Build and run. Now, the **cast** row slides in from the top while also fading into view.

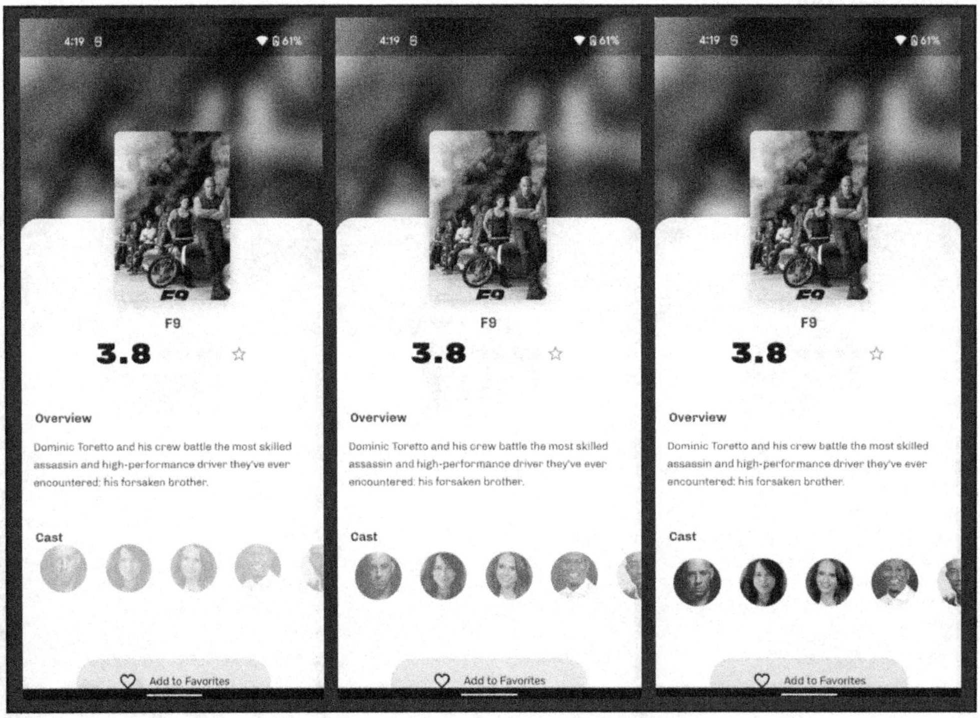

Excellent job adding your first Jetpack Compose-based animation! You can tell how low-effort this animation implementation was compared to the XML world.

Next, you'll improve the UX of the details screen even further.

Animating content sizes

In the app, a few of the movies have lengthy overviews. Unfortunately, these movies' overviews take up so much space that they push the cast row and the **Add to Favorites** button off the screen.

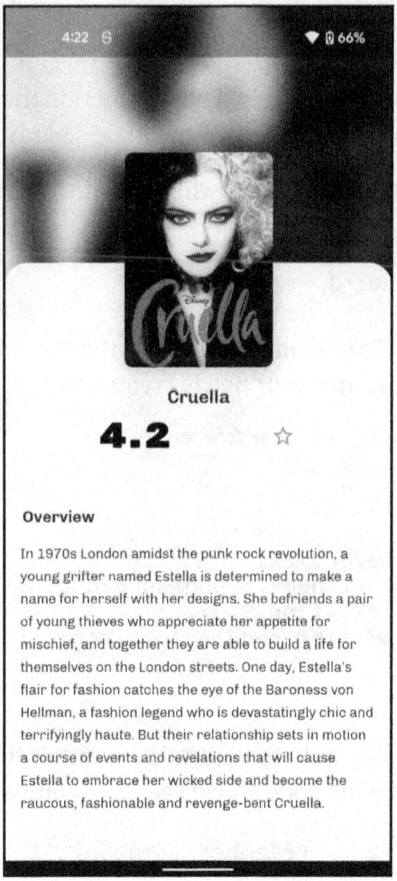

It would be better to restrict summaries to a few lines, so other sections of the UI remain visible. In addition, the user should have an option to expand the overview if they want to read more. You'll tackle this issue next.

Hiding and showing long text

Create a new file named **Overview.kt** in the components package and create a new composable function, `Overview`, that takes in a movie object.

```
@Composable
fun Overview(movie: Movie) {
}
```

Since the overview section will contain a bit of functionality of its own, it's best to extract it out to its own file to consolidate the logic cleanly in one place.

Open **MovieDetails.kt** and add the following line of code right above the line `CastRow(cast)`:

```
Overview(movie = movie)
```

Now, find and cut out the `Text` composable from the `MovieDetailsBody` rendering the overview. Then, paste it into your newly created `Overview` composable, as shown below:

```
@Composable
fun Overview(movie: Movie) {
    Text(
      text = movie.overview,
      style = MaterialTheme.typography.body2,
      textAlign = TextAlign.Start,
      modifier = Modifier.padding(horizontal = 16.dp),
    )
}
```

First, you want to add a basic state to determine whether the overview is expanded or collapsed. Add the following code above the `Text` composable:

```
var overviewExpanded by remember { mutableStateOf(false) }
```

`overviewExpanded` is a Boolean state with an initial value of **false**, meaning the overview will begin in a collapsed state.

Next, based on the character length of the movie overview, you want to show a toggle to expand and collapse the overview text. Add the following code below the `Text` composable that renders the overview:

```
//1
if (movie.overview.length > 200) {
  Text(
```

```
    //2
    text = if (overviewExpanded) "READ LESS" else "READ MORE",
    style = MaterialTheme.typography.overline,
    modifier = Modifier
      .padding(24.dp)
      .clickable {
        //3
        overviewExpanded = !overviewExpanded
      },
  )
}
```

You only want to show the toggle if the movie overview exceeds 200 characters — roughly four lines in the app.If the `overviewExpanded` state is `true`, the toggle should say **READ LESS**; otherwise, it should say **READ MORE**.When the user clicks the toggle, you need to change the value of the `overviewExpanded` toggle state.

Build and run. The newly added toggle now shows up for movies with lengthy overviews — and now, when you tap the toggle, the text changes.

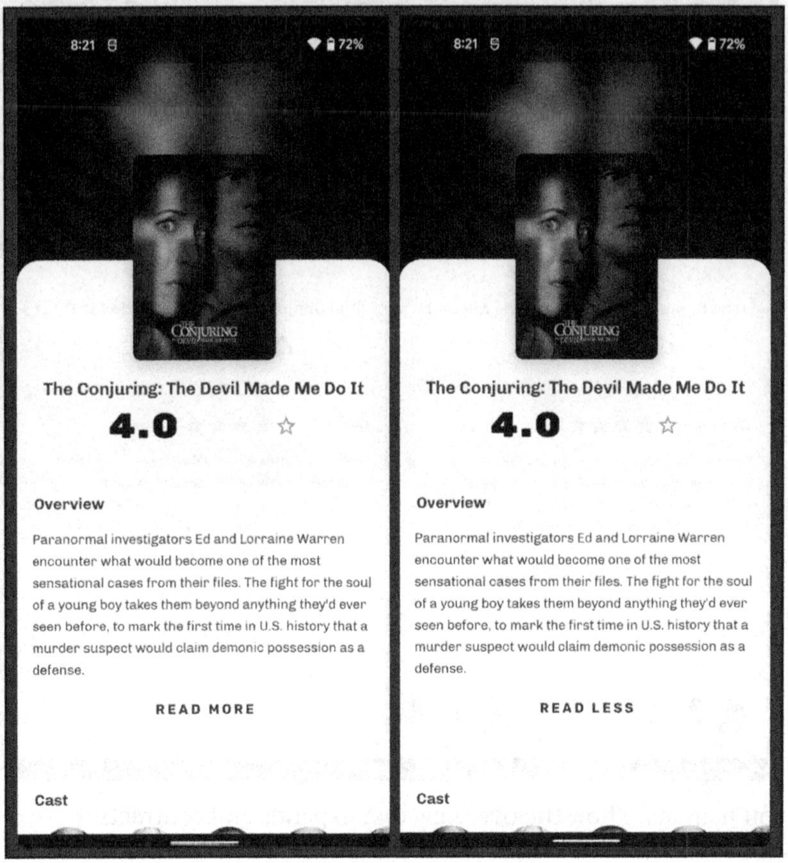

Now, you'll make the overview text expand and collapse based on the toggle. First, add the following `maxLines` property to the `Text` that renders the overview:

```
Text(
  text = movie.overview,
  style = MaterialTheme.typography.body2,
  textAlign = TextAlign.Start,
  modifier = Modifier.padding(horizontal = 16.dp),
  maxLines = if (overviewExpanded) Int.MAX_VALUE else 4
)
```

With the `maxLines` restriction in place, if the `overviewExpanded` state is `true`, the app will show the entire overview. Else, it will limit the overview to four lines.

Build and run. Now, tapping the **READ MORE** toggle will expand and collapse the overview text.

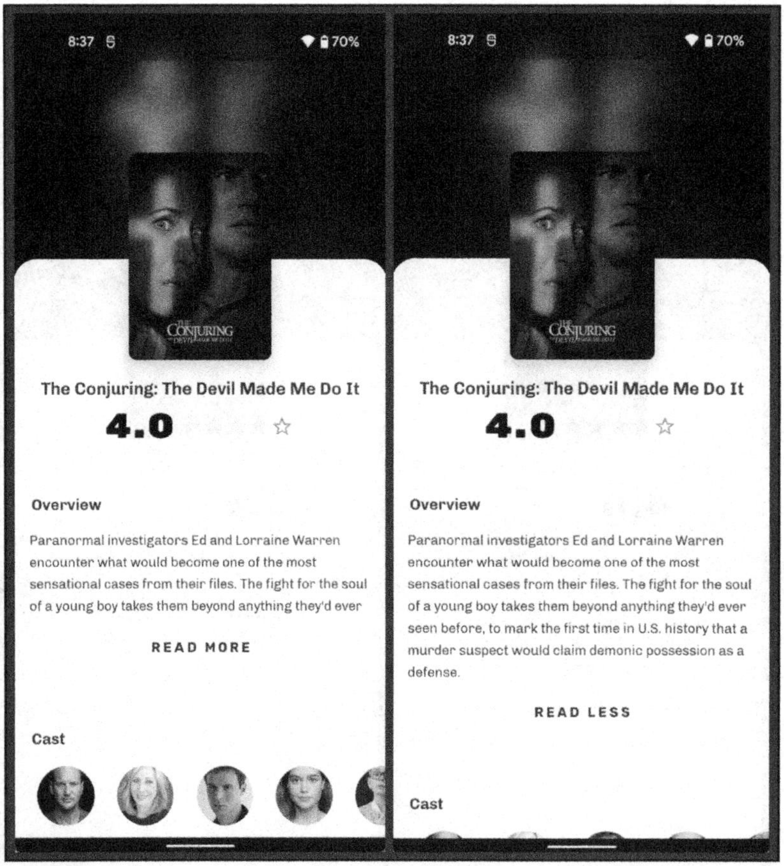

Finally, you'll animate how the overview text expands and contracts.

Animating the change in the text

Wrap both `Text` composables inside a `Column`, as shown below, to animate the text:

```
@Composable
fun Overview(movie: Movie) {
  var overviewExpanded by remember { mutableStateOf(false) }

  Column(
    modifier = Modifier.animateContentSize(),
    verticalArrangement = Arrangement.Top,
    horizontalAlignment = Alignment.CenterHorizontally
  ) {
    Text(
      text = movie.overview,
      style = MaterialTheme.typography.body2,
      textAlign = TextAlign.Start,
      modifier = Modifier.padding(horizontal = 16.dp),
      maxLines = if (overviewExpanded) Int.MAX_VALUE else 4
    )
    if (movie.overview.length > 200) {
      Text(
        text = if (overviewExpanded) "READ LESS"
               else "READ MORE",
        style = MaterialTheme.typography.overline,
        modifier = Modifier
          .padding(24.dp)
          .clickable {
            overviewExpanded = !overviewExpanded
          },
      )
    }
  }
}
```

The column you added has a special modifier attached to it, `animateContentSize()`, that animates the column's size when its child changes size.

Build and run. Now, toggling the overview text will expand and collapse the text with a fun little animation.

Wasn't that easy? Imagine achieving the same animation using views!

Next, you'll add an animation to the **Add to Favorites** button in the details screen.

Animating state changes

In the details screen of any movie, tapping the **Add to Favorites** button will bring up a circular progress bar that displays while the operation is in progress:

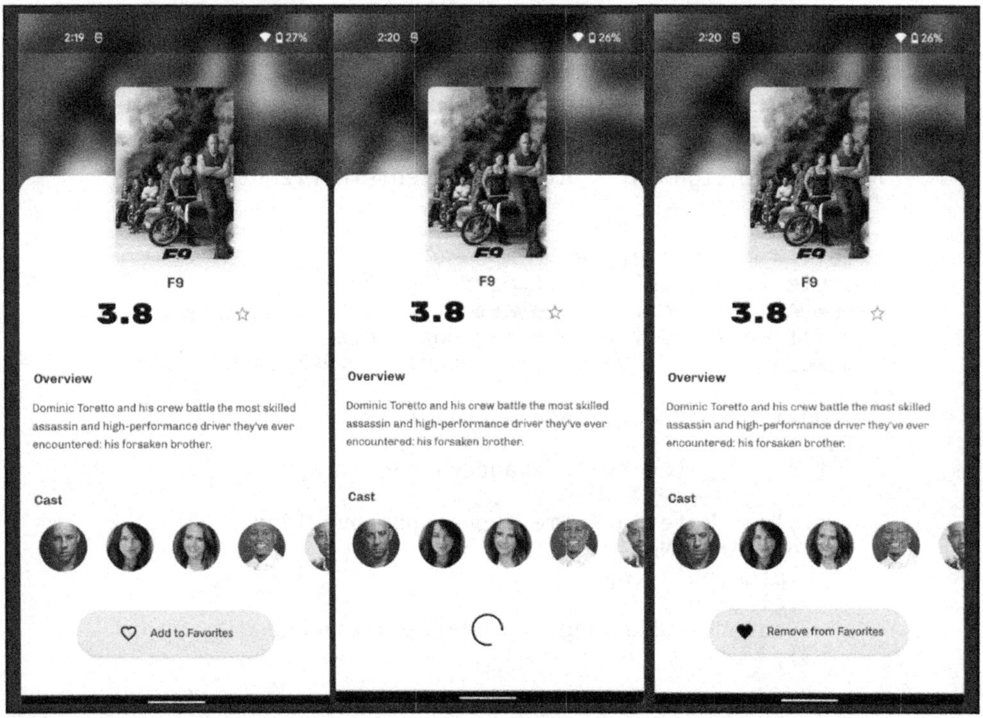

Since this feels pretty lackluster, you'll replicate the animation you added for this button in Chapter 2, "Animating Custom Views".

Before you can achieve the desired animation, you have to take care of a few things:

- Determine the visibility of the progress bar based on the loading state.
- Reduce the button width and hide the text and icon when the button is loading.
- Bring the button back to its original width, then show the text and icon when the operation finishes.

The button already tracks the loading state through the `contentState` property you passed to it as a parameter. Using this state's value, you'll trigger the animations. Jetpack Compose has a perfect candidate for use cases where multiple properties need to change depending on the state: `updateTransition()`.

`updateTransition()` sets up a transition based on the target state you supply. When the target state changes, it runs all of its child animation for its new target state.

Giving the button a state

To use `updateTransition()`, the button needs a state of its own. Open **AddToFavoritesButton.kt** and add the following `enum` to the top of the file:

```
enum class ButtonState {
  IDLE, PRESSED
}
```

This `enum` will denote the button's two states.

Next, add the following code to the `AddToFavoritesButton` composable, right after the `Column`:

```
//1
val buttonState = remember { mutableStateOf(ButtonState.IDLE) }

//2
val transition = updateTransition(buttonState.value, "Button
Transition")

//3
val width = transition.animateDp(label = "Button width
animation") { state ->
  when (state) {
    ButtonState.IDLE -> 250.dp
    ButtonState.PRESSED -> 56.dp
  }
}
```

In the snippet above, you create:

1. A mutable state instance called `buttonState` that has an initial state of `ButtonState.IDLE`.
2. A transition using `updateTransition()` that uses `buttonState` to determine the target state.
3. A width property using `transition.animateDp()`, which will toggle the value from **250dp** when in the `ButtonState.IDLE` state to **56dp** in the `ButtonState.PRESSED` state.

Toggling the button's state

Now that you've set up a state for the button, you need to add a mechanism for toggling that state. To do that, you'll use `contentState`, which `MovieDetails` observes and passes down as a property.

Add the following code below the width property declaration:

```
buttonState.value = if (contentState is Events.Loading) {
  ButtonState.PRESSED
} else ButtonState.IDLE
```

In the snippet above, the button's state will be automatically toggled when the `contentState` property changes.

With all the core pieces in place, it's finally time to animate the button.

Animating the button

First, get rid of the check that renders the`CircularProgressIndicator` when `contentState` is `Loading`. Remove the `if` statement starting with the following including the `else` portion, all the way to the } for the else:

```
if (contentState is Events.Loading) {
      CircularProgressIndicator(
        modifier = Modifier.padding(top = 8.dp),
        strokeWidth = 2.5.dp,
        color = Color.Black
      )
    } else {
    ...
    }
```

`CircularProgressIndicator` will now be a part of the button instead of rendering separately.

Now, move the `CircularProgressIndicator` inside the button, by placing the below code segment after the line `} else ButtonState.IDLE`:

```
Button(
  modifier = Modifier
    .size(250.dp, 56.dp),
  shape = RoundedCornerShape(32.dp),
  colors = ButtonDefaults.buttonColors(
    backgroundColor = MaterialTheme.colors.secondary
  ),
  onClick = { onFavoriteButtonClick(movie) },
```

```
) {
  Row(verticalAlignment = Alignment.CenterVertically) {
    if (buttonState.value == ButtonState.PRESSED) {
      CircularProgressIndicator(
        modifier = Modifier.padding(top = 8.dp),
        strokeWidth = 2.5.dp,
        color = Color.Black
      )
    } else {
      Icon(
          imageVector = if (movie.isFavorite) {
              Icons.Default.Favorite
          } else {
              Icons.Default.FavoriteBorder
          },
          contentDescription = null
      )
      Spacer(modifier = Modifier.width(16.dp))
      Text(
          text = if (movie.isFavorite) {
              stringResource(
                  id = R.string.remove_from_favorites
              )
          } else {
              stringResource(
                  id = R.string.add_to_favorites
              )
          },
          style = MaterialTheme.typography.button,
          maxLines = 1
      )
    }
  }
}
```

With this change in place, `buttonState` now determines the button's content. When `buttonState` is:

- **ButtonState.PRESSED**: The circular progress displays.
- **ButtonState.IDLE**: The icon and text display.

Changing the size of the button

There's one final thing to sort out before the animation is ready: To make the button shrink and grow, you need to use the `width` property you created earlier.

Replace the hard-coded **250dp** in the button's size modifier with the width property, as shown below:

```
Button(
  modifier = Modifier
    .size(width.value, 56.dp),
  shape = RoundedCornerShape(32.dp),
  colors = ButtonDefaults.buttonColors(
    backgroundColor = MaterialTheme.colors.secondary
  ),
  onClick = { onFavoriteButtonClick(movie) },
) {

    ...
}
```

With this last change, you've completed your animation. Build and run to see it in action.

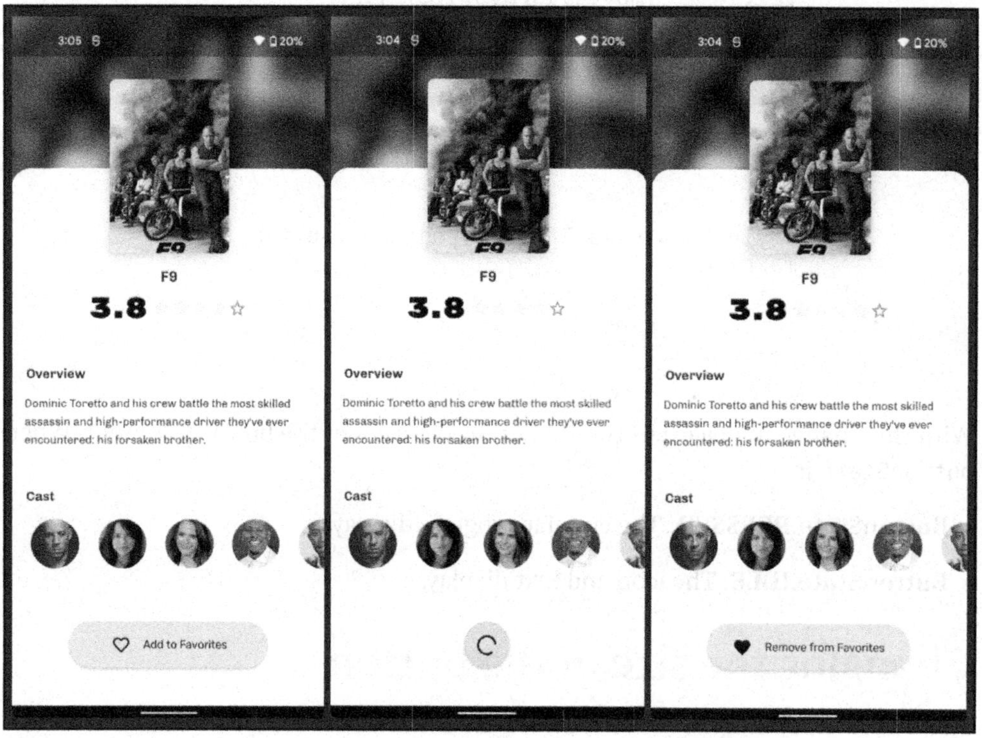

This animation is way more appealing. Best of all, compared to your original implementation, it's far less involved.

Challenge: Animating the button color

You animated the button width using the `animateDp()` extension available for the `Transition` in the button animation.

There are several other helpful extensions available for `Transition` that let you manipulate various properties across state changes. For example, `animateSize` animates both the width and the height across state changes, while you can use `animateOffset` to animate a composable's position.

As a quick exercise to flex your Jetpack Compose muscles, add an animation that will animate the button's color, as well as its size. You'll change the color from `MaterialTheme.colors.secondary` to `Color.Cyan`, based on the button's state.

For some visual aid, here is what that animation should look like:

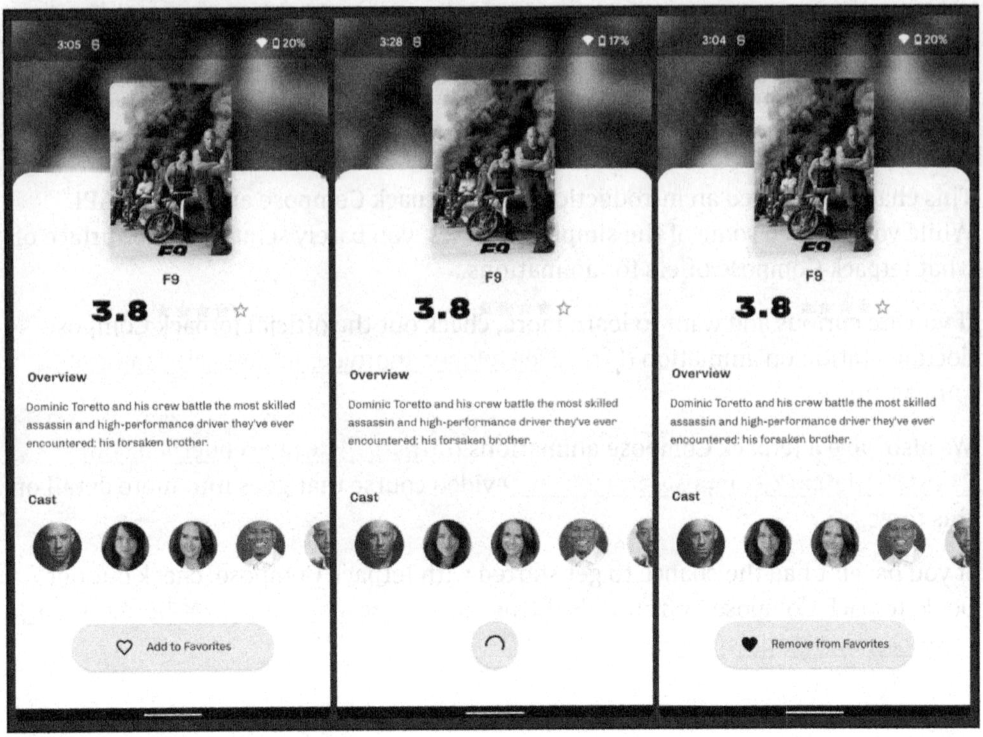

Feel free to check out the challenge project for a solution.

Key points

- Jetpack Compose introduces a comparatively simple set of APIs to add animations to your app.
- `AnimatedVisibility` lets you animate the visibility changes of a composable.
- `AnimatedVisibility` is still an experimental API at the time of this writing, so composables using this need the `@ExperimentalAnimationApi` annotation.
- To animate content size changes, use `animateContentSize()` on the parent container of a composable.
- To trigger based on state changes in your app, use `updateTransition()`.
- `Transition` has several convenient extensions. For example, `animateDp` and `animateSize` let you animate properties of a composable across state changes.

Where to go from here?

This chapter provided an introduction to the Jetpack Compose animations API. While you covered some of the simple use cases, you barely scratched the surface of what Jetpack Compose offers for animations.

If you are curious and want to learn more, check out the official Jetpack Compose documentation on animation (https://developer.android.com/jetpack/compose/animation).

We also have a Jetpack Compose animations (https://www.raywenderlich.com/21451892-jetpack-compose-animations/) video course that goes into more detail on this topic.

If you haven't had the chance to get started with Jetpack Compose, check out our book, Jetpack Compose by Tutorials (https://www.raywenderlich.com/books/jetpack-compose-by-tutorials/v1.0).

11 Conclusion

We'd like to thank you for joining us on this wonderful journey through the wide array of animations available to you on the Android Platform. Animations bring life and fun to your user interfaces and can provide critical cues to your users to gain their attention and give them a stunning surprise.

Now you're equipped with the tools to add all the important animation effects to your app, from subtle view animations, to transitioning between screens and animating lists and gestures, and even animating items when using Jetpack Compose. We hope you'll take what you've learned and apply it to your very own app to create memorable effects your users will love.

If you'd like to learn more about Android, we recommend *Jetpack Compose by Tutorials* to learn even more indebth about the features of the new and exciting Jetpack Compose. If you'd like to go even deeper into understanding the architecture of an Android app, we recommend *Advanced Android App Architecture* to get really sophisticated when architecting your apps on Android.

If you have any questions or comments about the projects in this book or in your own animations, please stop by our forums at https://forums.raywenderlich.com.

Thank you again for purchasing this book. Your continued support is what makes the books, tutorials, videos and other things we do at raywenderlich.com possible. We truly appreciate it!

Wishing you all the best in your continued journey on the ever evolving Android platform.

– The *Android Animations by Tutorials* team

Made in the USA
Monee, IL
05 November 2026

67977844R00122